Man of the House
A story about becoming a better man
by becoming a better father

by Kalkin Trivedi

Copyright © 2023 Mars Evolving
All rights reserved.
ISBN: 978-1-942711-03-2

Dedicated with love to my late wife. You gave me the gift of fatherhood. I am grateful. I'll remember you every day for the rest of my life, which I continue to spend looking out for our offspring during increasingly dangerous times, until the day I join you in death.

Notices

Although the author and publisher have made every effort to ensure that the information in this book was correct at press time, the author and publisher do not assume, and hereby disclaim, any liability to any party for any loss, damage, or disruption caused by errors or omissions, whether such errors or omissions result from negligence, accident, or any other cause. In plain English: you are responsible for the consequences of your own decisions.

There are references throughout this book to other books written by other authors. Make your own decisions regarding what to do with the information they provide.

The lessons in this book are conveyed through a fictional story. While some of the events in the book were inspired by real-life incidents, none of the characters in the story represent any actual people, living or deceased.

Mars Evolving
PO Box 16085
Seattle, WA 98116

Table of Contents

Preface..viii
Prologue...1
The incident...9
New friends...19
We interrupt this program...55
Trouble...71
Solidarity...101
Words & Feelings...117
Needed but not loved...145
New directions...199
Appendix I: Beliefs that cause trouble...................................245
Appendix II: Patterns that cause trouble.................................253
Appendix III: Situations that cause trouble..............................257
Appendix IV: Problem-solving techniques..................................275
Appendix V: Sample family rules..281
Bonus report: First steps in learning at home............................285

Preface

This section is an overview of what the book is about and how it came to be that way. You can skip it if you like, but it provides some interesting context. For this 2023 update, I've added some new twists and turns the book has taken as it's evolved.

I got the idea for the book after witnessing too many incidents like one that touched off the series of events in the story that follows this introduction. I thought that teaching parents how to discipline their children without assaulting them or screaming at them might make the world a better place.

As my ideas developed further, I started realizing that a lot of problems in our adult life have their origin in our childhood, when we didn't have enough experience to come up with better solutions to our problems then than the ones we did come up with. Worse, if problems that happen while we're growing up never get resolved, they get entrenched in who we become. In other words, even small problems in childhood can turn into big ones in adulthood.

I thought I could make the world a better place by applying my problem-solving skills to better parenting. I quickly ran into an obstacle: hostile feedback. Not "this is where I think you can improve"; it was more along the lines of "you shouldn't be *allowed* to publish this!"

Man of the House

Conflicting beliefs about parenting seem to draw heated emotional reactions as it is, and it didn't help that my ideas are in direct conflict with ideas circulating in feminist circles.

I decided to re-target the book to a friendlier audience, but that lead me to the next roadblock. The original title of an earlier version of this book was the recommendation of someone with some experience in copywriting who happened to have been someone of influence within paleoconservative circles. He's passed away since the original publication of this book. In honor of his legacy, I'll add some context that was missing from earlier versions of this book: he was a good man who passed along good ideas about business and career from the bro-net, and unfortunately also some bad ideas about family and parenting from predecessors and higher echelons of power.

I had sought out his advice because I'm neither a recognized authority nor a professional writer. When I explained the topic of the book, he told me he could not think of any possible reason I might write it.

His beliefs on the matter:

- Dads ARE utterly superfluous to family life, except to provide paychecks.

- He also believed that companies should have a preference for hiring women over men, because he claimed this would improve their bottom line, somehow. He was excessively optimistic about having enough scraps left over for male breadwinners; suffice to say in reality, there are not enough jobs to go around as the labor participation rate has been in a long-term downtrend especially for men.
- In other words, he thought the only thing you contribute is a paycheck, but then he left an insurmountable obstacle to your ability to accomplish even that!
- He thought dad SHOULD stay out of matters of child-raising, including discipline, leaving those matters 100% to mom, while he focuses his time and attention on his career. If something happens, he should tell mom and let her take care of it.
- He assumed boys SHOULD be raised in a female-dominated environment. He thought in terms of the Victorian dichotomy between the ruthlessly competitive masculine space of business and politics, and a gentle, nurturing feminine space of home, family, charity, and church. The latter space was supposed to be preferable for raising boys: feminine angels taming masculine devils.

I advise you to think differently. If you are superfluous, you'll be treated accordingly. You'll fare better making yourself indispensable.

More of his beliefs (not mine), to put matters into perspective:

- Marriage and family are primarily for the benefit of men because they "civilize" (sic) us. This argument is not particularly compelling to either feminists or women generally. It's effectively begging women to put up with husbands as an act of charity.
- Divorce is usually initiated by men abandoning their wives- for younger women. The only other common reason is when a woman is trying to escape an abusive husband. (note: these beliefs are not supported by relevant data)
- "If mama ain't happy, ain't nobody happy." In other words, to have a good marriage, a man needs to placate and defer to his wife (including but not limited to as regards child-rearing).
- Feminism per-se is a force for good, and we need more of it! The only problem has been a few well-intended but misguided radicals at the fringe. We need to save feminism from itself by nudging the radicals towards more productive directions and throwing our full support behind mainstream feminists.

Some problems happen because people create them as pretexts for hidden agendas. In the previous version of this preface, I compared his beliefs to those of a "radical" feminist and found that not only were their positions similar aside from superficial branding for different audiences, but his position was actually the more radical one. She was willing to positively asserted that fathers want to raise their own offspring, a problem from her point of view which she proposed to resolve through fatherless, collectivized child-rearing. He, on the other hand, never even considered whether men want to raise their own offspring or not because he didn't perceive any relevance as regards anything that mattered to him. Both takes were motivated by political, social, and economic agendas related to treating humans as livestock in order to maximize profits and concentrate power.

> "[Nicholas Rockefeller:] 'Aaron, what do you think women's liberation was about?'"
> "And I said...I had pretty conventional thinking about it at that point, and I said things about women having the right to work, getting equal pay with men, just like they won the right to vote. You know. And he started to laugh. "You're an idiot." You know. And I said 'why am I an idiot?' And he said 'let me tell you what that was about. We, the Rockefellers, funded that. We funded women's lib.' You know. 'We're the ones who got all over the newspapers, television, the Rockefeller Foundation. And you wanna know why?' He said there were two primary reasons: and they were one reason was we couldn't tax half the population before women's lib, and the second reason was now we can get the kids in school at a younger age...we can indoctrinate the kids how to think...this breaks up their family...the kids look to the state as the family...as the school...as the officials...as their family...not as the parents teaching them...and so those were the two primary reasons for women's lib..."
> —Aaron Russo, from Reflections And Warnings: An Interview With Aaron Russo

My advisor's admonitions didn't dissuade me from my plan to publish this book. His mental model of reality didn't match my experience; I remained convinced that I was on the right track because my critics had a lot to tell me but nothing to show me. My kids weren't the ones creating a ruckus in public or private spaces; they were happy, well-adjusted, and well-behaved.

Giving kids lots of attention and supervision was something we got right from the start. There was plenty more about parenting we had to learn the hard way, because the parenting practices that raised us were influenced by pressure to put career ahead of family. Making a living is important, certainly, but having a healthy way of relating to life and to other people is more critical for making a living than having egoistic notions of "career." In the case of my wife's family, it wasn't a matter of their own choices; she grew up in a communist society where work schedules were imposed on both her parents. She was often left alone, and her mother would take breaks from work at the hospital to pick her up out of her crib and nurse her. We both followed our instincts that told us children need more attention than what we got ourselves.

While writing this book, I kept discovering more things dads do, or could do, for their kids. Indeed, at this point, my brain is overflowing with ideas, to the point I'll run out of time before I can get them all down in books. It's increasingly obvious that androgynous parenting, with dads relegated to superfluous, junior under-secretary mom status, was a bad idea. Circumstances may vary, like ours did with our youngest, but generally your job is something along the lines of provide, preside, play, and protect.

> "When my grow up my be a mommy. When Daddy grow up he be a mommy too!"
> "I sure hope so, Teddy. That would be a huge upgrade for our family."
> —@momlife_comics

Sharing what I've learned is still a priority, but now it's imperative to rally the troops to action: there's a war being waged...

...against fathers
...against families
...against children

> **Representative Erin Healy** @RepErinHealy · Feb 13
> Extremist group Family Heritage Alliance said this morning that the safest place for kids are in families that have a married mom and dad. What a dangerous and un-American belief.

Bad parenting practices AND harmful influences in government, schools, media, social media, and religious institutions are creating conditions that promote

- depression, anxiety, and poor self-esteem, leading to outcomes like mental illness, drug abuse, and suicide
- beliefs and habits that hamper children's (later, adults') ability to relate well with others, leading to failed personal and business relationships, loneliness, and unhappiness
- gender confusion

This is a call to action, lads! Based on what I've witnessed, I fully expect most family lines in the "first world" countries to die out within a generation or two. If you don't want yours to be one of them, you'll need to take initiative and stand firm against social pressure, criticism, and even intimidation tactics.

The previous version of this book already had a lot of advice to protect your family from bad actors, but after some explosive revelations on social media I now realize that the abuses my own family had stumbled into were NOT a one-off; there's an entire activist network at work undermining parents and harming children. Whatever institutional systems had been in place to prevent the problem are now hopelessly broken and contributing to the problem. It's up to us to protect our families. I've updated some relevant advice here, and more may show up through other channels later.

The most recent twist in my personal journey as a dad was when, due to my wife's long battle with cancer, I became first the primary caregiver of our youngest offspring, and ultimately, a widowed dad. What came next was a fresh wave of doubts expressed as to my competence to raise a child, despite the fact that I've already been doing so and by their own admission there's nothing wrong with my youngest daughter. I would guess most of it due just to me being a man, and the rest to my obstinance in bucking popular trends I deem harmful. I don't care; I don't feel needy for approval, especially not from people who criticize my parenting style despite expressing disappointment at the outcome of their own. Don't tell me; show me.

Now it's story-time. I prefer not to deliver lectures because they're boring and don't sink in. Instead, I prefer to tell stories that convey vicarious life-experience, similar to the way our ancestors shared hard-won wisdom through stories told around the camp-fire.

Presenting the lessons as a story is my idea, and typical of my way of doing things, but credit for the advice itself goes to many others. None of it is my invention; I'm just passing along what was shared with me after making some intelligent assessments of the quality of the advice, and observing what actually worked in practice with my own kids. Most of it comes from therapy and applied psychology, and all of it based on science and practice; none of it is based on political or social agendas imposed from above.

I hope that you enjoy the story, and I hope that you find your own adventure as a dad as enjoyable as I did my own. They were the happiest moments of my life.

Kalkin Trivedi,
Seattle, WA

Prologue

Jason Olson had a promising future.

His dad, Dr. Carl Olson, was a respected oncologist at a local treatment center world-famous for the advanced state of its cancer care, as well as a lecturer at a prestigious medical school. His mom, June Olson, volunteered in the local public schools and maintained an active social life.

He had two older brothers. Todd, the oldest, left the nest a few years after Jason was born. He remembered hearing a lot about him, though: his teams won trophies in crew and in swimming. Todd was in demand in the old-boy network and had a good job representing a highly-profitable, privately-held, high-tech company.

Middle brother Doug had confined his athletic pursuits to odd games of racket-ball, but he made it through a grueling computer science major, and got a coveted internship at a hot local software company. He scored a technical lead position fresh out of college, and soon thereafter, a wife close to the top level of management.

There was a substantial age gap between his older brothers and Jason; he was a late-life surprise. That meant that he had financially well-established parents and two successful older brothers to hear about and live up to their examples.

The Olsons were well-respected members of their social circle. Carl and June were considered a model couple, and the

Olsons were frequently referred to as a "good family." Carl was generous with his son. June often told him how lucky she was to have him, considering he arrived after she thought she couldn't have any more children.

By his early teens, Jason had a lot of unspoken assumptions about life. He expected to go to college, find a good job, start a family, and with them enjoy a standard of living comparable to what he was used to growing up.

Then one day after supper, June casually announced that she wanted a divorce.

There was no scandal involved. She neither had a boyfriend nor had any suspicions or concerns that her husband might be cheating on her. There was no abuse, and not even any arguing. The money Carl brought in afforded the luxury of allowing both himself and June to pursue their personal interests without having to compromise and work out common priorities. June didn't seem to be angry with Carl, nor had he given her any particular reason to be. All June had to say about the matter was that she no longer wished to be married.

In order to fund the divorce settlement, the Olsons had to sell the family home. June used the proceeds to buy two condo units in a new building jutting out over the water on a pier; one to live in, the other to collect rent from so that she didn't need to draw down her net worth for living expenses. Both units had spectacular views. The building was part of a complex that included some cafés and restaurants, including one popular with the local ladies who lunch, and a small but very convenient mini-mall. A whole marina was wedged around the complex, there was another next door, and a park on the other side with

Prologue

views of sea and sky. June had some experience sailing as a teenager and quickly found herself in demand at the local yacht-club as a crew-member for sailing trips, some of them extended and all of them quite luxurious. She got to share the lifestyle of wealthy bachelors, divorced men, and widowers without having to marry one.

Carl downsized to a smaller, more modest house in the same general part of town as the previous house, but in a somewhat less wealthy neighborhood further from the lake. He lost the gated entrance, lake view, and quick access to the private waterfront, but the new house had a nice deck for parties and a pleasant view of the immediate neighborhood, and it was a little closer to his beloved university. He wanted to salvage as much of his accustomed lifestyle as he could after June left him to start a new one of her own.

If there were any custody agreements for Jason, he was unaware of what they might have been. It didn't seem to be on the minds of either of his parents, and neither one talked to him about how the divorce would impact him.

June's condo had only one bedroom. When Jason stayed with her, he had to sleep on the sofa. Then he started noticing that everything he did was wrong. It began as nagging, then turned into constant, irritated criticism. His mother would come home in a good mood that quickly soured by his presence. He thought he'd teach her a lesson by staying at his dad's full-time until she asked him to come back. To his surprise, she not only didn't, but seemed immensely relieved.

It seemed to him the problem was solved. Everything was fine for a few months. Then one day, his dad brought home a nurse who'd had her eye on him for a while. Carl saw a new relationship with a significantly younger woman as an opportunity to transform his fiasco with June into a gift from the heavens. Introductions were brief, and Jason had the impression he was expected to make himself scarce for the rest of the evening.

She spent the night.

After that, she came and went, but spent increasingly more time in Carl's home. On those nights Carl would hastily suggest activities designed to keep Jason out of the way.

Eventually, she moved in full-time, and Carl approached Jason for an awkward conversation that never got to the point. Carl seemed to have difficulty expressing himself. Jason had a feeling that the point that never materialized was to get Jason to commit to a new level of making himself scarce.

The feeling was reinforced when he found himself and a core set of belongings dropped off at Todd's house out in a distant exurb community. It was just 5 o'clock in the afternoon when they arrived, so just before he left, Jason's dad told him to expect his brother to return home shortly.

Jason ended up spending that night on the back porch, shivering, his head on his backpack as a pillow.

When Todd and Jason eventually connected, Jason got a key, which enabled him to sleep indoors.

Todd's house was situated in a "lifestyle community" featuring an artificial lake and an irrigated golf course out in the middle of what was otherwise a barren landscape. The nearest services were all down the freeway about 10 miles, by design. All the houses looked alike; their color schemes were regulated by the community association, which also banned fences and any landscaping other than the modest foundation plantings around the bases of the houses, and the lawn that flowed between the houses unbroken, both professionally managed by a crew of immigrant laborers in uniform, who mowed the lawn and sprayed chemicals on it.

Todd's house served primarily as a repository for his toys, but was otherwise somewhat superfluous to his lifestyle, which involved a lot of traveling on business and living out of hotels and restaurants. Before he left again, he gave Jason free rein to help himself to food, entertainment, and anything else he might need anywhere in the house. Todd was, after all, Jason's big brother, even if they didn't know each other all that well.

The next morning Jason looked for some breakfast. The huge, double-door, stainless steel refrigerator contained four packs of microbrew beer, one bottle each of ketchup, mustard, and relish, a jar of mayonnaise, some green olives, and a jar of maraschino cherries. The freezer contained some mixers for alcoholic drinks and two-thirds uneaten portion of a pint of an upscale brand of ice-cream.

Jason ate the ice cream and wondered what he was going to do for lunch and dinner. He lay on the sofa a long time, then eventually turned on some music. He listened for a few minutes, then turned it off, feeling vaguely uneasy and not knowing why. Later in the afternoon, needing something to distract himself from his own thoughts, he turned on the cable television.

He stumbled onto something interesting. His heart raced with a mixture of excitement and guilt. He'd never seen pornography before. It consisted of a series of fetishes, some of which he found disturbing. After five minutes, he turned it off, disgusted.

Half an hour later he turned the television back on again, this time looking for something other than pornography. He watched something else for twenty minutes before he could no longer stand the feeling that he was watching a feature-length commercial announcement. Then he tried flipping through the channels. He kept trying for some time despite not finding anything worth watching. He finally turned it off, sat moping for a while, then made his way to his brother's bedroom, closed the door, pulled down the blinds and drew the curtains to darken the room as much as possible, crawled into bed fully clothed, and pulled the pillows and blankets around his head to shut out the world. That's where he spent the rest of the day and a sleepless, hungry night.

The next day he got busy on the phone. Thankfully Todd had an otherwise extraneous VOIP phone service that came with the cable and internet.

His dad would have sent money if asked; unfortunately, he wasn't answering. Unbeknownst to Jason, he was entertaining his love interest in the French countryside. At the moment they were bicycling on a back-road lined with chestnut trees, somewhere in the Auvergne, on their way to a supper of stuffed partridges and assorted braised seasonal vegetables.

Jason didn't want to bother his mother because it would just upset her. What he didn't realize was that this was not an option anyway as she too was incommunicado at the moment while examining the fascinating coral reefs off Belize.

Prologue

He got through to Doug, but Doug told him he couldn't talk and would call him back later when he had time. Apparently, he didn't have time for the rest of the day. Jason wondered, justifiably, if Doug were a workaholic. The next day he tried again, late enough in the day that even if he was still at work, he might reasonably justify taking a few minutes to talk to his brother, but early enough that he would still be awake. Doug sounded a bit abrupt, but after scolding Jason for not having a job, agreed to send some money. A few days later a crisp $100 bill showed up in the mail with a sticky note attached saying "love, Doug."

Jason looked for a job online and sent around some resumes and cover letters. Only one of them got a response, which wasn't surprising as jobs for teenagers had become essentially obsolete, and half of the listings Jason fell for were solely for the purpose of feigned compliance with regulations in order to hire contractors on H-1B visas. A lot of walking and hitchhiking got him to the job interview. The manager he met did all the talking for a few minutes, didn't ask any questions, and shook Jason's hand as he escorted him to the door. It took a couple days to get back to Todd's house.

Jason had not finished high school, and right now, his grades were tanking because he wasn't showing up at school. He was vaguely aware that he had the option of taking a G.E.D. He talked to a financial aid counselor about college, who hinted that while he could apply for loans, grants and scholarships were out-of-the-question because he didn't "qualify." He was also discouraged by the fact that he didn't feel ready to take any college entrance exams.

He was living on ketchup mixed into hot water as "soup," crackers enclosing mayonnaise as "sandwiches," and drink mixers diluted with water as "juice." All of these items were running low. He'd already eaten all the olives and maraschino cherries.

It was early evening, and the days were getting long. He wandered out of the house and looked out first over the golf course, where he spent some time watching two elderly couples playing, and then turned his gaze to the lake, watching the boats for a long time, until it finally got dark.

He went back into the house and flopped into bed, fully clothed. The next morning, in a sudden burst of energy, he tidied up the kitchen, the bathroom, and the recreation room, and made his brother's bed.

Three months later, Doug was the first to notice that nobody knew where Jason was.

The incident

"¿**C**uando podemos comer?" (when can we eat?) asked a little boy about four years of age. He wasn't misbehaving but looked dangerously on the edge of getting fidgety.

Trays of food, still wrapped up, had been set up on a folding table set against one of the walls. His father wondered what it was and how long it would keep at room temperature.

"Tenemos que esperar a los demás invitados," (we have to wait for the other guests) answered his mother, holding a baby girl in a sling. Her light-brown hair had one natural blond streak right down the middle of her French braid. She looked European, but behind the times, as if she had walked out of the 1950s in her light minty-green soda-shop dress and white knee-high stockings.

They were all were sitting on folding chairs at one of the tables in the room, whose windowless walls were undecorated. It looked like a seldom-used meeting room in a complex that bore a strong resemblance to a suburban office park. The owners called it a "resort" and did a brisk business in weddings and parties.

"I know it's been a long wait for you," said his father after a few moments, "and I appreciate how patient you've been. If other guests don't show up soon, I think we might just eat and leave."

His wife looked over at him with some concern. Truth be told, Dad was getting impatient too.

He felt relief from the frustration and embarrassment that were weighing on his mind when he heard another group approaching the room. It was his sister-in-law, one niece who looked to be about six, and another niece who appeared to be in her mid-teens.

His relief was short-lived. The mother entered the room looking tense. He had a bad feeling. Within seconds, his hunch was confirmed.

"I don't like this food!" exclaimed the girl almost instantly after spotting the trays.

"You haven't even seen it yet," said her mother in a rush of words as she hurried to start unwrapping a tray. "I want you to have a look first before you decide."

"I SAID I DON'T LIKE THIS FOOD!" repeated the girl, even louder than before, as if she'd already grown impatient with her mother's deafness. "I WANT MAC AND CHEESE!"

"STOP IT!" yelled her mother. "This isn't a restaurant; you can't just order whatever you want! Look they have drumsticks..."

"I DON'T WANT DRUMSTICKS. I SAID I WANT MAC AND CHEESE!" shrieked the girl, stomping her feet.

The little boy's attention was now focused on her, and his eyes were widening in shock. "Why is she acting like that?" he asked his dad in English.

"Hablaremos después," (we'll talk later) whispered his dad, starting to blush as the girl's mother glared at him.

The incident

"Knock it off! If you won't eat the drumsticks, then you'll just have to go without," she snapped at her daughter as soon as her attention returned to the matter at hand.

The girl gritted her teeth and reached for the platter of chicken drumsticks. Her mother started saying "DON'T YOU..." but it was too late: the drumsticks were hurled against the wall, splattering it and the table with sauce, while the drumsticks and the platter ended up scattered all over the floor.

The woman lunged at the girl and grabbed her by the hair. "LEAVE ME ALONE," the girl shrieked as she clawed at her mother's hand, and then she swore.

The woman slapped the girl hard in the face, then punched her twice in the shoulder. There were a couple of gasps, and the boy's father looked pleadingly over to a stocky man who just walked into the room.

"THAT'S ENOUGH!" the girl's father bellowed.

His wife shot around to confront him. "If you don't like the way I discipline her, then why the hell don't YOU ever do anything? You ALWAYS leave me to have to deal with her!" she yelled, shaking the girl for emphasis.

"I SAID THAT'S ENOUGH!" he repeated, stretching himself to his full height to look more intimidating. Then he went over and grabbed his daughter, whose convulsions settled down quickly into heaving sobs as she threw her head against his chest. "I'll take her back to the hotel," he said.

As he turned to leave, the girl looked over her father's shoulder, then stuck her tongue out at her mother, who, for her part, answered with a threatening motion as if she were about to charge.

Instead, once the girl disappeared around the corner, the mother sighed deeply and collapsed into a chair.

There was a long, awkward silence.

Now that the younger girl was out of the picture, the teenager attracted some attention.

She was tall, slender, and had a single long, thick, amber-colored braid going down the back. She had a pretty face and was wearing a bit of make-up. Gold-colored wire-frame glasses with elliptical lenses sat on her nose.

At the moment she was getting herself some food. It took a long time. She finally came to one of the empty tables the furthest from where everyone else was sitting, with exactly one chicken drumstick and a big piece of chocolate cake. She went back for some fruit punch. While she was away from the table, the little boy sat down at a place setting right next to hers. When she came back, she glared at him but said nothing until after he did.

"Do you like fruit salad? I do..." he started chattering in English.

She turned to him with her eyebrows furrowed. "Why are you talking to me?" she said with an icy edge to her voice.

He didn't take the hint and kept chattering. Luckily his dad did take the hint and rescued him before the hostility escalated. He brought him over to his own table and put him between himself and his mother. He went back to grab his son's food, and tried to avoid exchanging glances with the offended teenager. Luckily there was no risk of that as her attention was now solidly absorbed by a book she had brought along. She picked absentmindedly at her plate, at a slowing pace that suggested

The incident

she wasn't going to finish what little there was.

At the other table, the smattering of "would you like some butter?" and "more coffee?" gradually turned into real conversation.

The mother's name was "Barbara."

She was a marketing manager at a major software company, just below executive level. Graduated magna cum laude from an avocado-league university.

As her mood improved, so did her social sophistication. Not surprisingly for someone of her rank in life, she was a skilled conversationalist. The adults at the table talked at length about various people they knew in common. Barbara provided perspectives on their careers, while the younger mother holding her daughter filled in the details regarding marriages and children.

Meanwhile, the children were getting tired and bored. The teenager eventually walked out of the room without so much as a friendly wave good-bye, while the boy started fidgeting, and the toddler girl began fussing.

The girl's mother checked her diaper, then tried to soothe her to sleep, while the boy's father tried coaxing him into sitting still a while longer.

"You know, you ought to read this book I've been reading about parenting. It's by Pandora Hightower, the child development expert. Made the best-seller list in parenting. She's absolutely brilliant," Barbara offered helpfully. "I'll send it to you."

The young father looked around for a piece of paper, while his wife looked anxious. He took one of the cards that had been used to label one of the buffet items, then scribbled his address, phone number, and email. He wondered if Barbara were raising her daughters using the Hightower method.

It was getting late. It would be bad enough driving back to the city in the dark, with two sleepy kids. And they hadn't even greeted the guests of honor yet.

When they expressed their intention to say their good-byes, along with apologies for leaving so soon, Barbara just rolled her eyes. "Don't expect a warm welcome to the party. I'm pretty sure that not inviting us to the wedding and then banishing us from the main reception hall were part of a plan."

It turned out that Barbara's suspicions were correct. "I specifically asked that children NOT be brought to the reception!" shrieked an almost skeletally thin woman with bleached-blond hair when she spotted the two children. "What an inconsiderate ass you are! You've ruined everything!"

"Nobody told me anything..." the young father tried to say in his defense before getting interrupted.

"It was right on the invitation!" she screamed, as if he were deaf—and quite stupid.

"We didn't get a written invitation, we were invited..." he started to say.

"THEN WHAT THE HELL ARE YOU AND YOUR BRATS DOING HERE?" she shrieked.

He tried to find diplomatic words to express that he and his family were present at the invitation of the man who had paid for both the wedding and the reception, but before he could squeak out more than a few words, a tall, muscular man grabbed him roughly, told him to "JUST SHUT UP!", and tugged him in the direction of the door. He offered no resistance.

The big man, who happened to be the groom, escorted the family to the parking lot. "Not now. I'm in enough trouble as it is. I'll talk to you about it later." He grabbed the young dad's hand, squeezed it so tight it hurt, and gave it a few shakes. That was it for "Hello, so nice to see you again after all these years, good-bye now!".

It was a long and quiet drive back into town. He suspected that his wife didn't understand quite what had happened but must have realized it was something unpleasant. Truth be told, it wasn't something that he wanted to talk about, nor did he think he could actually explain it. She was as sleepy as the kids, so she never got around to asking any questions before dozing off to sleep. She awoke when the sound of the engine was replaced by one of opening and closing car doors.

They were parked in front of a 1910s cottage that had housed several generations of fishermen and their families, surrounded by a crowded neighborhood of similar modest homes. The current owner was not a fisherman, but he had worked all his life until a late retirement at the shipyards. He was one of a dwindling number of older blue-collar residents, most of his generation replaced by a younger crowd who moved in fresh out of college.

Getting into the house quietly with sleepy children so as not to disturb him at midnight was a nerve-wracking challenge, but once they all piled into the bedroom, there were sighs of relief.

Dad was ready to just take the shoes off the boy and tuck him in, but mom didn't want him to cut corners, so she took charge of getting him properly ready for bed.

Eventually, everyone was tucked into bed. Although groggy, Dad managed to make up a bedtime story about a robin and a pair of pesky chipmunks, then gave everyone in the family a hug and a kiss. He hoped he would drift immediately into sleep after that, but instead, ended up brooding for hours.

Something was terribly wrong, but at this point, all he knew was that his current experiences were not matching up with his mental model of what family life was supposed to be like. He realized that the divorce that turned his life upside-down didn't just happen; there must have been causes that preceded it. But when he tried to scan his memory for clues as to what went wrong, first of all, nothing came to him, and second, something else he didn't understand was bothering him and clouding his mind.

The only thing that was starting to occur to him was that the kind of family he grew up in was not the kind he wanted for his children. He wanted them to feel love, protection, and security. But the only thing Jason felt sure of was what not to do.

About dads and bedtime stories:

> *It is remarkable that paternal bookreading, not maternal bookreading, predicted story comprehension, book knowledge and language skills among children. Gleason (1975) and Bernstein-Ratner (1988) reported that fathers used more complex language than mothers when interacting with their children (Bernstein-Ratner, 1988; Gleason, 1975). More recent studies found that paternal vocabulary but not maternal vocabulary was a*

significant predictor of child language (Pancsofar & Vernon-Feagans, 2006). A previous study with a sub-sample of this EHS sample demonstrated that fathers used more non-immediate talk during during bookreading interactions with their children (at child ages 24, 36, and five years) than mothers (Duursma & Pan, 2011). Non-immediate talk goes beyond the context of the book and is known to have an effect on children's language development (De Temple & Snow, 2003). If indeed the fathers in this study similarily used more complex language than the children's mothers, this could provide a mechanism by which their bookreading may have influenced children's language and emergent literacy skills.

—The effects of fathers' and mothers' reading to their children on language outcomes of children participating in early head start in the United States

Anna E. Duursma

University of Wollongong

eduursma@uow.edu.au

New friends

The next day Jason was in a better mood. The plan was that after work he was going to stop by home to take a quick nap and freshen up so that he'd be presentable, then drive to the airport to pick up a couple arriving from London.

He'd met the husband at the bus stop a few months earlier. He was friendly and chatty. One day the bus's wheelchair lift jammed at their stop, putting them both at risk of getting into serious trouble at work for being late. Jason told him to follow him back to Jason's house, where they got into Jason's car. He dropped him off at his work before arriving at his own employer and spending more than he could comfortably afford on all-day parking.

He rescued the wife a few weeks later when she was stranded at a client's house late at night, not realizing that due to a holiday she wasn't aware of, bus service to that neighborhood ended before her babysitting shift was over.

After that, the husband asked for a ride to and from the airport. They were a tad helpless at times, but affable and very polite.

Jason couldn't honestly call them "friends," but he was eager to make new friends ever since his precipitous fall from rich-man's son to "poor relations" rendered him *persona non-grata* with all but one old chum named Ryan, and even he didn't seem to have much time for Jason anymore. He had in mind a plan to invite them to supper before sending them home. He had a feeling that his offer of hospitality would be more compelling to them than the alternative of showing up in their own apartment tired and hungry.

The drive to the airport didn't go as planned. Jason had assumed the forty-five minutes he'd allocated for travel would be enough, because he was going to take the old airport road that most out-of-towners didn't know about. It had a few stoplights on the way but never jammed up like the freeway did. Unfortunately, it took longer to actually get to the old airport road than he expected, and then traffic was heavy in the vicinity of the airport itself.

The next matter of concern was the matter of the actual arrival time, and how long it would take them to get through security and customs.

He decided he'd better park the car and look for the couple at baggage claim. The kiosks there would tell him about the arrival time, which would give him a closer guess as to where they were in the process.

It took longer to park than he had guessed, and then it was a long jog to the terminal.

He arrived at baggage claim thoroughly flustered. What a way to make an impression on guests!

He took a quick look around the immediate vicinity, then looked for one of the arrival-departure kiosks. He spotted one and quickly scanned it. Their flight number wasn't listed, so he waited for the next batch. He searched carefully through those, and still couldn't find it! The kiosk alternated between only two batches of flights, so Jason assumed he must have missed it on

New friends

the first batch. He waited for that bunch to display again, but didn't see it, then double-checked the next batch one more time, only to conclude that the flight simply was not listed.

He had no idea what that meant.

His mind raced. Vytautas was fairy fluent in British School English. Birutė had a smaller vocabulary and a non-native accent, but was functional, if a bit shy. They were unlikely to have significant cash on themselves, much less be willing to part with it, and were therefor unlikely to wander away from the terminal on their own.

Jason was determined to find them. He might have to check at the airline's desk to see if someone could explain to him what happened to the flight from London. Maybe scour the entire baggage claim area from one end to the other. In the meantime, the pressure on his bladder was unbearable in his current nervous state. He sought out the nearest public restroom.

Jason did his business, then headed out in a hurry. There was no door, just a blind corner for privacy. Turning the corner in a rush he managed to collide head-on with another man who was hurrying the other direction.

Jason was winded but left standing. The other chap was in worse shape, being the smaller of the two. He had bounced off Jason and landed sprawled out on the floor, arms outstretched in a futile attempt to catch onto something to break his fall. He took quite a spill, but due to his modest size did not hit the floor with enough momentum to do much damage. His luggage had flown out of his hands, tumbled onto the floor, and burst open, scattering his clothes.

The man's attire was more-or-less hipster: skinny navy-blue jeans, sky-blue and copper plaid button-down shirt, whose buttons matched in size and shape but not color, and a muted red-purple sunset tie tied in a curious-looking Eldredge knot. His pale, boyish face sported a groomed stubble-beard, which was too light-colored to be particularly conspicuous. Somewhat short hair, stylishly tousled on top, neatly trimmed at the edges, completed the picture.

Jason stood looking at Vytautas in wide-eyed surprise. Vytautas looked back a bit stunned at first, but then a good-natured grin began curling on his lips.

Jason smiled nervously back and offered an arm. Vytautas grabbed hold of it, then allowed himself to be pulled to his feet again. He and Jason then began scrambling for Vytautas's scattered belongings. Some were getting trampled on, including a pair of undershorts that got caught on a lady's high heel. She impatiently tried to shake it off, but instead managed to work her foot into it. She then tried shaking all the harder but couldn't get it off. Apparently she did not want to touch it.

"Excuse me, ma'am, do you need some help?" offered Jason sheepishly. She had the kind of doll-like face that looked cute when angry, but she held her foot still for a moment. It was attached to a shapely leg, exposed by her short, neatly-tailored skirt, and dressed smartly in fashion stockings. Jason quickly disentangled the offending garment, blushing deeply.

Jason turned to Vytautas, who had finished picking up the rest of his belongings, though he was still a bit disheveled from the fall. Still grinning, he nodded in the direction of the quickly departing lady and winked.

Jason grinned back for a moment, but then his subconscious alerted him that his attention was needed elsewhere. A young woman was approaching with a bewildered look on her face. Birutė matched her husband's modest size and elfishly child-like looks. She was dressed more conservatively than her husband, in a neatly-tailored coffee-bean colored skirt to her knees, matching jacket and narrow-rimmed pillbox hat, and pink blouse. Her blond hair was managed in twists on the sides, ending in a loosely-twisted chignon in the back. Jason flashed a grin in her direction to reassure her that everything was OK.

Vytautas quickly set down his luggage so that he was ready to grab Jason's hand as he approached. He pulled it towards himself, then grabbed Jason's shoulder with the other.

"Evening, Jason," he said casually. He and Jason broke into laughter simultaneously as Birutė joined them, smiling pleasantly.

It turned out that Vytautas had just been through hell. None of it Jason's doing; they'd arrived early, both gotten molested by TSA, then Vytautas was strip-searched and interrogated after wisecracking "don't I get drinks and dinner first?"

His jovial mood despite what happened was infectious, so Jason forgot all about the fiasco with his late arrival and Vytautas's poor treatment. It just felt good to have some company for the evening.

The dining-table had been folded down and set over on one end of the day-room, where a single cabinet with a small sink, countertop, and built-in half-height refrigerator served as the kitchen. It was the sort of all-in-one mini-kitchen unit you might see on boats or in tiny foreign apartments; this one handmade judging by the choice of rustic materials and styling. The owner preserved the woodwork with an occasional coating of boiled linseed oil, the way his grandfather had taught him. Supper had come out of a multi-pot sitting on the end of the counter.

The other end of the day-room now served as a spot to relax and entertain guests after supper. Coffee, tea, and slices of Obstkuchen—a simple German-style cake—covered in glazed tropical fruit were distributed here and there on plates and saucers sitting on doilies, wherever there was a convenient spot, for lack of a coffee-table. Pots and pans dangled from pegs on the walls on the cooking end of the room. On the walls of the sitting end were hand-tools suspended from hooks, and an old cuckoo clock straight out of the Black Forest.

Vytautas was rolling around on the floor, rough-housing with Kai.

Jason felt a strange mixture of emotions: a warmed heart seeing the spirited play, but also a sense of shame. Was this how other dads played with their kids?

Jason wasn't imprinted with this kind of behavior. He searched his memories and could find none of either of his parents ever being playful with him.

He looked over at his wife Veronika. She had a warm, dreamy look on her face as she watched the action from her rocking chair, looking down from time to time to see how Kaarina, their toddler daughter, was doing.

Jason shuddered, wondering if Veronika were making comparisons between himself and Vytautas. He wanted his kids to be happy and feel loved. He made up his mind to learn some games to play with his kids.

Veronika mentioned something to Kai about his audition for a children's talent show, so after a lull in the action with Vytautas, he ran off to get his quarter-size guitar. Jason fetched his son's stool. Kai came back with his guitar and started performing.

The budget was tight for formal lessons, so Jason gave Kai lessons himself using what he remembered from his own lessons, and his old music books for beginners. They were short ten or fifteen-minute sessions right after dinner.

Kai was learning fast, perhaps not too surprising because of the consistency of the lessons. What was more impressive was that Kai could sing. He had perfect pitch, an intuitive sense of the mood of the song which translated into the right dynamics for both his playing and singing, and a surprisingly husky voice for his age. It was the kind of cute but also somewhat impressive performance that would get a lot of attention on social media had anyone been posting it.

The show over, Jason suddenly started becoming aware of the late hour, and wondered when Veronika would start getting anxious about the time.

It turned out that he'd read her thoughts accurately, but her mood was relaxed and lenient. She told her son to put away his guitar and gave him five minutes warning that it would be time to get ready for bed. Kai groaned but did not put up a fuss.

The old man sitting in a chair next to Jason's, stroking a cat sitting on his lap, looked disappointed too. That was Herbert, the owner of the house they lived in. Although he had retired as a machinist at the shipyards, he was neatly groomed and had genteel mannerisms. Never smoked or swore like most of the rest of his work crew did. Veronika took care of shopping and meals for him, and Jason pitched in when he needed physical help. He turned the whole house over to them except for his own sleeping quarters, and gave them a deep discount on rent for looking after him.

Since the fun was over and it was past his own bedtime anyway, Herbert excused himself. Jason asked Vytautas to wait while he escorted Herbert to his bedroom, which was right next to the day-room where they had all been visiting. The cat trotted ahead and was already waiting inside when he got there. Once Herbert was transferred from the walker to the bed, he assured Jason that he was fine and bade him not to keep the guests waiting. He was being polite, but it was true that he could manage by himself. Ironically, the issue of being a good host reminded Jason of his obligation to be a good care-taker. He lingered a few moments, looking around the tiny room that was more of a sleeping nook than an actual bedroom, being barely longer or wider than the narrow bed. It was all Herbert wanted or needed.

The book. The glasses. Jason fetched them and placed them to within Herbert's easy reach. Herbert smiled and thanked him, and confirmed that he would probably read for a few minutes because that was, in fact, his usual habit. He put on the glasses, made himself comfortable, then reached for the book, while the cat made herself comfortable on his belly.

Jason closed the door behind himself and rejoined Vytautas who had been patiently waiting alone. The kids had already been prepared but it would take Veronika a few more minutes to get the children settled down and asleep. Birutė was with her, mostly watching but also helping. Vytautas and Jason heard a bit of scolding and grinned.

They patiently waited for Veronika and Birutė to return before starting any real conversation. They took a detour through the kitchenette to pick up some cups and pots of coffee and tea.

After they arrived at the table, Veronika asked how his parents were. "Oh, they're very content," Vytautas answered. "The UK was the promised land for them."

"Yes, but it must have been hard on them too...I mean, leaving all their family behind," said Veronika a bit wistfully. She had an indistinct accent when speaking English, making it hard for strangers to guess where she was from.

Vytautas sighed. "I don't know. They never talk about it. They do send some letters back home though."

Jason for his part was eager to move the conversation away from the topic of dying relationships. "Well, tell us about London, then! What did you do while you were there?"

The question must have seemed absurd to Veronika. She viewed the world through her own expectations, and assumed that Vytautas would have been doing the same sorts of mundane domestic activities that she did when visiting relatives. For her, the only point of travel was to maintain long-distance relationships...like when a cousin she'd never met before arrived from Russia.

Vytautas's eyes lit up, however. He obviously had something interesting to talk about. "Ah, well, I got in four days of seminars with some of the biggest names on Harley Street!"

Veronika gave him a blank look. He must have correctly interpreted it, for he filled in the missing context without further prompting. "Harley Street, ah, that's where many of the best doctors in the UK have offices."

"You're studying to become a doctor?" asked Veronika.

"Oh, no, not just physical healers there," answered Vytautas. "Harley Street is also where some of the best hypnotherapists in the UK have clinics. I attended a hypnotherapy seminar."

"What's hypnotherapy?" asked Veronika.

"It's about using hypnosis to help people solve their problems," explained Vytautas.

Vytautas read the look on her face and must have realized he was getting himself in trouble. He might have thought of Veronika as being a "German girl", but things were a little different in South America. More like the Mediterranean countries, where what little familiarity the cultures have with hypnosis has sinister associations tied to it, like giving someone "the evil eye."

"Ah, it's just a way of talking to people to help them work out their own problems," he explained. "People often think of their mind as being a single monolithic entity, but actually it has many working parts that sometimes get out of alignment. For example, we often have intentions to do one thing, but impulses to do something else that sabotage those intentions."

Veronika looked at him skeptically. "Well, isn't that just a lack of discipline?"

"I don't know," said Vytautas. "Tell me more about what you mean."

"I mean, when you're a child, your parents teach you how to behave, and if they teach you that something is wrong, you won't do it," she answered. "But if they don't teach you that when you're young, then you end up having to learn the hard way when you're an adult."

"That's very interesting," replied Vytautas. "I'm curious about how the process goes wrong. Do you suppose that there are times when the parents had the intention to teach their children how to behave, but the children don't learn...perhaps because the parents are unconsciously sabotaging their own intentions and training children the wrong way?"

Veronika and Jason suddenly exchanged glances. Now Vytautas's curiosity was aroused in earnest, and he pressed them to tell him what they were thinking.

Jason sighed, then related the details of the incident involving his younger niece Angelina and his sister-in-law Barbara at the resort. He didn't bother to mention the sullen behavior of his older niece, Aimée, though in the back of his mind he was worried about that too. Vytautas listened intensely, while Birutė looked troubled by what she heard.

Vytautas remained quiet and pensive-looking for many seconds after Jason finished speaking, until Veronika challenged him: "What would a hypnotist do in that situation?"

"In what role?" asked Vytautas. "As an onlooker?"

"As the parent handling the naughty child," specified Veronika.

"Oh, good, because that's an easier question. Well, first of all, if that were my child, the misbehavior is unlikely to have happened in the first place," he said.

Veronika looked at him skeptically. "Well, why not? How do you know you wouldn't have a naughty child like that one?"

"I want to make sure I understand the question, so please bear with me," replied Vytautas. "Are you assuming that the problem is with the child? Well, I suppose the problem is certainly being transferred to the child, but the way I look at the situation, the problem starts with the parent.

"It wasn't the child who put herself in the situation; it was her parents. It was also the parents who decide how to react to her behavior, and that determines whether the behavior is encouraged or discouraged. If their children's behavior is a problem, the parents need to change their own behavior first."

Veronika looked startled for a moment, then thought about it, and said: "Well, I see that the mother over-reacted, but by then she was angry and frustrated."

"That's right; she was angry and frustrated," said Vytautas agreeably. "Like I said, she was the one with the problem. She reacted to the girl's behavior by getting angry, instead of by doing something rational to solve the problem. Admittedly the girl got angry and frustrated as well, but that's because her mother ignored what she wanted and kept trying to force her own way. It helps if you at least consider and respect the child's point of view."

Now Veronika looked scandalized. Jason had a feeling that she wasn't sure if maybe she was being baited, because what Vytautas was telling her was apparently outside of her expectations. "Now wait a minute!" she objected. "The problem started when the little girl was rude and shouted at her mother."

"Hmm—well, you're right that rudeness is unacceptable," Vytautas agreed. "So, then, why didn't the mother address it? Why get angry about an unacceptable situation, instead of staying calm and doing something about it?"

"Well she did do something, she..." Veronika paused suddenly as a look of confusion spread over her face. She left her sentence unfinished.

Vytautas helped her out. "That's right; she assaulted the girl. She lost her temper after several attempts to ignore the problem and hope the girl would comply, instead of addressing the misbehavior directly."

"Then...what should she have done...to correct the misbehavior?" asked Veronika.

"Well, for starters, you promptly interrupt it," he answered. "Then you calmly give feedback, meaning a warning, a reprimand, or consequences, depending on the situation and the severity of the offense.

"In this case, a warning to stop the rude behavior. Because the girl hadn't previously been trained to respond to warnings, she would probably have continued mouthing off, at which point she should have been escorted out of the room before the situation escalated."

"That sounds right to me as well," agreed Birutė, who was trained as a nanny. "There is no point in arguing, pleading, or reasoning. Just tell them what you want them to do, and if they disobey a direct order, then calmly assign consequences."

"You make it sound easy," said Veronika skeptically.

"Well—yes—everything's easy when you do it the right way instead of the wrong way," said Birutė matter-of-factly. "Think about the difference. In one case, the parent is doing roughly the same thing over and over again—arguing, pleading, reasoning, or threatening—but expecting a different result! Nothing changed until the mother lost her temper, and that only made matters worse.

"Now think about how things could have been different if she had given a command, and then switched tactics just as soon as the command was ignored. If she had changed what she was doing, the result would have been different."

"In the first case, there's nothing to discourage the misbehavior," said Vytautas.

"But the mother did punish the girl," objected Veronika. "I mean, it was brutal, but it was punishment."

"Yes, it was punishment," agreed Vytautas, "but for what? What do you suppose the girl associated it with?"

There was no answer, so Vytautas continued. "What the daughter is likely to associate the punishment to is not her own behavior at all—but instead, to her mother's bad mood! In fact, most punishments backfire because of the way the parents implement it. For example…" Vytautas hesitated, blushed, and then continued "when I did something wrong, my parents used to say, 'Come over here!', and if I did, they spanked me! Can you imagine what the effect was?"

Veronika looked puzzled, but Jason couldn't help but grin. "They were punishing you for obeying them," he answered. A look of amazement came over Veronika's face as the realization hit her.

"That's right," said Vytautas "There are a lot of cases like that where punishments or for that matter rewards backfire. It's because most parents have a poor sense of how artificial incentives work. For one thing, it's not like the child or for that matter even an adult is consciously reasoning his way through the situation. Most of our patterns of behavior are like reflexes. We don't really plan them.

"The rules that govern our patterns of behavior are simple. If you follow the rules they work; if you don't, they don't work. The child's conscious mind is not involved in the process, and it's not going to fix your mistakes."

Vytautas reached for his cup. Veronika noticed that it was empty, and poured him some more hot green tea. He thanked her, and then continued the conversation.

"Another mistake is to assume that the severity of the punishment must be related to the severity of the offense," he said. "Actually, it has more to do with balancing out the pleasure of achieving whatever the mischief was intended to accomplish, which means that most of the time mild feedback like timeouts work just fine, and eventually the warning is sufficient."

Veronika's maternal ears thought she detected a sound from the bedroom. The conversation stopped for a few seconds as she listened carefully. Nothing happened. The baby was still asleep. Veronika relaxed, and the conversation resumed.

"Now, there is a way to associate consequences to the girl's own behavior, and to give a fair warning before assigning them," Vytautas said. "When consequences are handed out, you remind the child why. That helps connect the warning with the consequences, so that eventually just the warning is enough.

"It's a lot like training animals. At first, you give the animals treats, and make a clicking sound while giving the treat. Once the animal unconsciously associates the clicks to the treats, you can hand out the clicks as rewards instead of the treats, and the animals will respond to the clicks just like they responded to the treats. Similarly, when assigning consequences, you remind the child of the warning you gave so that an association is made between the warning and the consequences. You might say for example 'I told you to give me the DVD. Instead, you threw it against the wall and shattered it. Now you sit in the corner until I come to get you'. The child will associate the warning to unpleasant feelings, so that in the future, the warning is usually enough."

Vytautas ate his last bite of Obstkuchen, then continued. "The other principle by which this strategy works has to do with managing habit formation.

"A habit is a repeated pattern of behavior that has a trigger, a behavior, and a reward. For example, a smoker might feel nervous—that could be a trigger for smoking. He reaches for a cigarette and starts smoking. That's the behavior. His reward is the effect of the nicotine on his body chemistry. It might also be the relaxation of taking the smoking break, though oddly enough it's not the smoking break that does it—he programs himself to relax whenever he gets the smoking break by creating a self-fulfilling expectation.

"Most of our behaviors are habitual. For example, when you wake up in the morning, you don't consciously plan what you're going to do in the next 45 minutes, you just get up and do whatever you habitually do after getting up in the morning.

"The whole morning pattern is a habit, and it's made up of smaller habits like how you shower, how you dry yourself, how you put on your clothes. Chances are, you're not thinking about how to do all those things, they just sort of happen automatically while your conscious mind is occupied with other matters. The part of your brain that manages habits takes over and does it all for you while your conscious mind is thinking of other things."

Veronika nodded knowingly. "And they had better be good habits, not bad habits."

"That's right," Vytautas agreed. "Our lives consist largely of habits embedded in habits embedded in habits. So this is why it's important to interrupt misbehavior before it turns into a habit.

"Now I already told you that a habit consists of a trigger, a behavior, and a reward. Take away any one element, and the habit isn't a habit anymore.

"Taking away the trigger is when you realize that a certain situation tends to trigger misbehavior, so you avoid or change the situation. For example, if boredom triggers misbehavior, a wise parent might bring along a book or toy along to a boring activity.

"Interrupting the misbehavior takes away the behavior, and handing out negative feedback diminishes the reward."

Veronika had a thoughtful look on her face as she nodded. "Well, it came to being sent away anyway. I suppose it would have been better to do that before the mother lost her temper."

"Unfortunately, that's a typical pattern," said Birutė. "The parent says 'stop it!', the child continues misbehaving, the parent argues, the child continues misbehaving, the parent makes a threat, the child continues misbehaving, then finally, SMACK!"

"That's the pattern because parents mistakenly believe that their children consciously choose their actions," explained Vytautas. "That's not true; they're repeating programmed habitual patterns. Scolding and threats are nothing more than noise they've gotten habituated to."

"But why didn't my niece anticipate what was coming?" Jason wondered aloud. "Given how bad their rapport is, I would guess they've had many battles."

"A better question might be why her mother didn't anticipate what was coming, and negotiate a deal before the heat of the moment," observed Vytautas. "The child's ability to anticipate what was coming was distracted by a desire to punish and manipulate the parent. That's probably the 'reward' that encourages the naughty habit."

Jason was lost in thought for a few moments before speaking. "It still seems counter-intuitive...but it's consistent with what I've seen. After she already got a severe smacking, my niece deliberately provoked her mother again as she was being taken out of the banquet room. She just couldn't leave it alone."

"Did her mother respond to the provocation?" asked Vytautas.

"She sure did," answered Jason. "Almost went after her, and I suspect if there weren't witnesses and if my brother hadn't been holding her at the time, she would have whaled on her some more."

"So the mother did respond to the provocation. Who, then, was in control of that interaction?" asked Vytautas.

"The daughter," answered both Jason and Veronika almost simultaneously. They looked at each other with a look of sudden realization.

"Who should have been in control?" asked Vytautas.

"The mother," they answered in unison.

"And specifically, the reasoning, problem-solving part of her brain, not the emotional part," added Vytautas.

"Now that you've explained it, it makes more sense to me," said Jason. "It seems there are always reasons that things turn out the way they do."

"Yes, there are always reasons, just beware that human nature is to find reasons before fully understanding the problem," warned Vytautas. "Parents often act on false assumptions.

"One of their false assumptions is that children are 'bad.' Children don't make plans to create trouble; they're simply acting according to an instinct to seek pleasure and avoid pain. In doing so, they often ignore the boundaries their parents unrealistically expect them to recognize without having learned them first.

"When parents mentally model their children's behavior as 'bad', without any consideration of the child's perspectives and motivations, that makes it hard for the parent to anticipate the problem or respond appropriately."

"Yeah, my sister-in-law seems to rationalize her own behaviors," said Jason. "Doesn't seem to think she's doing anything wrong. Truth be told, she's confident enough in her parenting style to recommend a parenting book."

"Which one?" asked Birutė.

Jason didn't remember the name of the book off the top of his head. "I'll show you," he said. He got up and went to the bedroom to fetch the book. He came back to the table, and handed the book to Birutė as he told her it was by Pandora Hightower.

She took it, then gave the front cover and back cover a thorough look before skimming through the pages. "I take it you haven't read it," concluded Jason.

She shook her head. "Didn't really learn my skills out of books," she murmured distractedly. "It was all a few lectures, some hands-on training for first-aid, and then a supervised practicum."

She stopped perusing the book and looked up at Jason. "What do you think? Worth reading?"

Jason knit his eyebrows and pursed his lips. "To be honest, I'm having a hard time slogging through it. It's not a pleasant read."

Birutė raised her eyebrows. "What's the problem?"

"It's kinda creepy," answered Jason. "It explains how to take care of infants and children, but using a very clinical style of language that would make more sense when explaining how to prepare a bacterial culture than how to take care of your own flesh and blood. It's like the author has no emotional attachment to the subject matter. Maybe she doesn't. She has a PhD, but no husband or kids."

"Hmm," murmured Birutė, "Might be a bad sign for the quality of the advice."

Jason sighed. "I'm having a hard time figuring out what exactly we're supposed to do aside from keeping them fed and changing their 'nappies.' It's all about taking care of physical needs, but doesn't seem to address anything about their feelings. On the contrary, we're supposed to ignore those."

"How so?" asked Vytautas, raising one eyebrow.

"Well, for example, we're supposed to keep them in a different bedroom than our own, which isn't even an option in this house," answered Jason. "And if we hear them wake up crying in the night, we're supposed to ignore them and let them cry it out. She's rather adamant on that point. But Veronika and I just don't have the heart..."

"Good!" interrupted Birutė, looking scandalized. "You're not supposed to! Don't you think your parental instincts exist for a reason?"

Jason felt abashed at the mild reproof. But then he realized it was more likely addressed to the author of the book, not him, and it was only because she was trying to warn him away from an idea she considered harmful to children. Still, he wondered if he hadn't been foolish to ignore his own misgivings regarding the author's opinions because of her status as an expert.

Vytautas knit his eyebrows and shook his head. "There's a longstanding meme going on in academia about 'child development'," he said. "The idea..." [he pronounced it the English way, "idear"] "...is that human children are like highly-bred bedding Petunias: just keep 'em fed and watered on a production schedule, and they bloom when it's their time, like clockwork."

He closed his eyes briefly and shook his head again. "That's not how it works with sentient, sapient beings. It's a more interactive and intelligent process. They'll never develop competence without learning, and to jumpstart that process, you have to build an engaging relationship with them."

Something was starting to click in Jason's head. "I wonder if career-oriented yuppy parents reading books like this one is how you get perfectly capable six-year-olds still wearing diapers."

"Tip of the iceberg!" said Vytautas. "It's the cause of the whole delayed maturity business that's been hitting all the first-world countries for generations now. Compare with traditional societies. Little girls in rural Africa routinely take care of toddlers, while western courts have ruled that a twelve-year-old can't be considered responsible enough not to bash a toddler's head against the wall. You have thirty-year-old man-children who can't change a flat tire much less earn a living, while a ten-year-old Amish boy helps his twelve-year-old brother replace a broken fence-post and secure the barbed wire."

"Well, that's what you notice on the outside," Birutė said gravely. "But think about what's going on inside. The emptiness they feel."

"Our relationship to our parents is a blueprint for future relationships," explained Vytautas. "Children who don't have healthy relationships with their parents aren't learning how to relate well. Nor do they develop a healthy interior narrative to displace all the unhealthy messages they hear in darker corners of the world."

Jason sighed, partially out of relief. "Well, then, no point in spending any more time on that book. I'll give it away to a thrift store."

Birutė gave him a serious look. "It would be better if you burned it. Do you really want to put bad advice in someone else's hands?"

Jason was startled by her remark. He hadn't thought the consequences through. Then he came to his senses. "You're right. Especially not when there's a risk of starting a domino effect for all eternity. I'll throw it in the paper recycling."

It was getting late for coffee, but Jason couldn't resist the urge to pour himself half a cup.

"Given the way she handled that incident, maybe my sister-in-law isn't really the best source of parenting advice," mused Jason after taking a sip of the coffee. "Not that I mean to criticize her, especially under the circumstances."

"You mean her being so stressed?" asked Veronika.

"Yeah," Jason answered. "Doug told me they might need someone to take care of Angelina for a while. I took that as a hint and told him we'd take charge of her as needed."

Veronika's face reacted with what looked like alarm. With a small child in her arms most of the time, she didn't need a spitfire like Angelina to add to her burden. Jason tried to reassure her. "It's not that they need us full-time. They're planning to hire a nanny. It's just that even with a nanny they can't count on her to be available at odd times and on short notice."

Veronika's mood suddenly brightened, but probably not because she felt reassured about being committed to being available at odd times and on short notice. She turned to Birutė and said excitedly "Birutė, you could apply for the nanny job! That would be perfect!"

Birutė looked right back at Veronika, and her eyes lit up too.

Veronika looked expectantly over at Jason. "OK, OK," he said, "I can pass a referral along to my brother, not that I have a lot of clout with him. But Barbara will almost certainly be the one who makes the decision. You'll have to play to her."

Review

Children are not "bad"; they seek immediate gratification and avoidance of pain. They're acting on impulses and habits, not conscious decisions.

Parents have to set appropriate boundaries for their children's behavior to prevent them from harming themselves or someone else, and they have to enforce those boundaries. Rules do not enforce themselves.

If you ignore, argue, yell, or try to reason, misbehavior is likely to continue past the point at which you lose your temper. That's a common way that abuse happens. You're less likely to lose your temper if you respond immediately to misbehavior consistently and predictably.

If you allow yourself to get angry, it will cloud your own reasoning and problem-solving ability, and trigger either fear or anger in your children. Then they get into the habit of reacting to problems with emotions that cloud their own reasoning and problem-solving ability.

Parents who ignore their kids while they're behaving, but give them attention when they misbehave, are giving them a perverse reward for misbehavior.

Promptly interrupt misbehavior, then give feedback in the form of a warning, a reprimand, or consequences, depending on the severity of the offense. Interrupting the misbehavior prevents it from turning into a habit. Habits are hard to break.

Habits are averted by avoiding the trigger, interrupting the behavior, or taking away the reward.

You can't always avoid situations that trigger misbehavior, but if you anticipate them, you can negotiate deals beforehand. That's often enough to prevent or at least mitigate trouble.

If misbehavior continues after a warning, interrupt it and give feedback in the form of nonviolent consequences.

Being sent to a corner (smaller children), being made to stand against a wall, temporary loss of use of a favored toy, and being banned from fun activities are all useful and adequate consequences for most problems. Just like any other animal, humans do more of anything that gets them a reward, and less of anything that comes at a cost. This is a true fact that can be objectively-verified in a laboratory, without regard to any ideology, beliefs, or labels. This book was written to teach you to work with this fact, without any violence or abuse, instead of against it, in order to maintain

> family harmony.
>
> This is appropriate for an early stage in your children's lives. At a later stage, they're going to have to learn to override artificial, and often purely psychological, rewards and punishments, any time those incentives conflict with real-life future costs and benefits.

The dad effect

The dad effect is the name for all the collective benefits of growing up with a dad at home. It includes lower rates of poverty, depression, mental illness, suicide, substance abuse, crime and delinquency, and under-age sexual activity among young people. It's easy to find references to it, but much harder to find documentation about specific things dads actually do that cause it to happen, so that we can do more of that.

Part of the problem is that the dad effect has largely been written-off by many sociologists as being strictly a function of contributing more income, so that fathers can be replaced by social welfare programs. The influential conservative I mentioned in the Introduction shares this belief. Many people want it to be true so to have a pretext for expanding the government, and also to reduce resistance to expending breadwinners for foreign policy objectives. It's obviously a wrong assumption, because some of the specific benefits, like kids developing bigger vocabularies when their dads read to them (vrs mom or nobody), are impossible to explain away in terms of income, especially given that the researcher specifically studied lower-income families. It's even harder when you zoom in on all the outliers, like working-class single dads who don't rack up the rates of social problems associated with single moms.

I'm not a sociologist, and I don't have a complete answer. I do have some partial answers, and some suggestions for where to start looking for answers:

- Dads are men. Relating to their dad teaches kids how to relate to future husbands, bosses, business partners, and any other man with whom they might need to transact. Kids who grow up without fathers seem to have difficulty relating to men in general, which adversely impacts their success in life.
- Dads play with their kids more than moms do. Oddly but not surprisingly, while doing research to find out what the benefits of playing with dad are, some of the first articles I found frame this phenomenon negatively ("dads play with the kids while moms have to do all the shitwork" sic!). One of the first resources I found that was actually relevant was a video of Dr. Warren Farrell claiming that rough-housing is significant, especially for boys (hence my cover-art). It has to do with appropriately controlling and channeling aggression, building empathy in order to accurately estimate how much you need to hold back with a smaller and physically weaker playmate, engaging physically as a precursor to learning how to engage socially (in other words, kids who get physical-contact play tend to be more socially competent), as well as some body-brain training and

coordination. If you're not imprinted with this behavior, here's a book with ideas: *The Art of Roughhousing: Good Old-Fashioned Horseplay and Why Every Kid Needs It*, by Anthony T. DeBenedet MD and Laurence J. Cohen PhD
- Dads have different communication styles than moms. Probably not actually better, but just being different opens up the possibility of benefits not conferred elsewhere. In particular, it confers a big benefit when dads read to their kids, a phenomenon I cover elsewhere in this book.
- Dads discourage potential child abusers and sexual predators, a phenomenon I cover elsewhere in this book.

Here's something else, and it's important:

> *We are fish who grow up in a small pond and even when we dump out into the larger ocean, we generalize those early patterns onto the world around us and expect it to conform to our expectations.*
> —Author and attachment specialist Adam Lane Smith, personal communications

We learn how to relate to other human beings when we're relating to our first caregivers. Those first relationships become the blueprint for other relationships for the rest of our lives. In addition to relationships with others, we also have a relationship with ourselves; we're also talking about "self-esteem" (in the best sense; NOT in the sense of children being taught to repeat self-praising affirmations). If there's trouble in the beginning, it usually persists for the rest of our lives.

The first person we relate to is usually mom, though sometimes it's someone else when she can't be the one. Here are some ways dads can improve mom's ability to bond to and relate to her babies:

- Either earn enough money, or be willing to take a hit to your standard of living, to allow secure attachments to develop before she returns to work (years, not days).
- Arrange your lifestyle to minimize the use of institutionalized child-care. Organize your lifestyle around your kids, not vice-versa!
- Make sure someone is responding to infants. Moms tend to have more instincts in that regards than dads do (dads tend to relate better to older children), but that instinct is getting dulled. Respond to infants and toddlers *as if* you're having a conversation with them. Not responding to infants' bids for attention causes all sorts of trouble, including delayed speech.
- Watch mom for signs of stress or anxiety and nip those in the bud with care, attention, and your own good mood. *Make this a high priority; this is a point of failure where things go wrong.*

Here are some ideas for how dads can relate well to their sons and daughters on their own part:

- Make a habit of allocating time and attention to your kids, including infants.
- *One of the most important things you could ever do as a dad*: maintain a friendly, appropriately-affectionate rapport with

your kids as your default way of relating to them*.
- When children misbehave, address the problem in a calm, businesslike manner, then promptly re-establish rapport once the situation is resolved.
- Get down on their level and look children in the eye when talking to them.
- Seek to understand and respect their points-of-view, then make your own understood.
- As children mature, you'll go from God's representative on earth to "all too human." Don't freak out; just maintain a good rapport with them as it happens.
- Train yourself to maintain a calm, imperturbable baseline mood.
- Physically play with them. Schedule playtime regularly, preferably daily.
- Recruit them for projects to work on together.
- Talk them through negative emotions.
- Don't end conversations with problems; end them with solutions and a commitment to implement them.

As of this writing, I've been reading a book about the epidemic of "narcissism" in the sense of self-obsession on the one hand and lack of consideration for the rights and needs of others on the other. The authors seem to understand the problem quite well, better than I do certainly, but their proposed solution is off-target. Something about "balance" between the old-school of parenting (aloof and overly authoritarian) and the new-school of parenting (indulgent and negligent). What the authors are unwittingly recommending is striking a balance between outcomes of self-loathing and neediness on the one hand and narcissism on the other.

A balance between two mistakes is also a mistake; the solution is on a completely different axis. Bully-wimp relationships are never ideal, regardless of whether the dad is the bully (old school) or the wimp (new school).

Wimp-dads tend to be socially-insecure men. One problem or the other propagates from generation to generation by either lack of intervention in abusive or negligent situations (passive or absent dad) or by being overly-indulgent, the latter often intended as compensation for spending too much time at work (which often enough is itself the result of a bully-wimp relationship between the boss and dad).

A friendly rapport with your offspring is not indulgent, and indulgence isn't friendly. You don't maintain indulgent relationships with your friends; you maintain mutually-respectful relationships (well, at least I hope so, though I am aware that some men with poor self-esteem do get themselves into bully-wimp relationships and call those "friendships" for lack of knowing any better).

Behold the power of AND: maintain a friendly rapport AND address misbehavior in a calm, business-like manner AND give attention, not "stuff" they don't need. If you follow this simple advice, that should avoid problems at both sides of the false dichotomy.

Here is a short list of things adults do to encourage narcissism:

- Give babies and toddlers physical care but not enough emotional & social engagement.
- Flatter kids for what they think they "are": you're so smart! You're so talented! You're so pretty/handsome!
- Give kids narcissistic role models, typically personalities associated with commercial entertainment or social media.
- Allow others to encourage over-confidence in girls, on the mistaken assumption that will contribute to their success without any drawbacks: "GIRL POWER!" "GRRLZ RULE!"

Here is a short list of things adults do to encourage self-loathing:

- Neglect babies and toddlers.
- Criticize or otherwise verbally abuse kids, especially for what you think they "are": How could you be so stupid! Stop crying, you stupid brat, or I'll give you something to cry about!
- Fail to rescue kids from abuse outside the home they don't have enough experience to handle themselves.
- Allow kids to be exposed to role models, either in real life or via commercial entertainment or social media, who model poor self-esteem.
- Allow others to attack boys' self-esteem. "Boys are stupid; throw rocks at them" (slogan on a t-shirt that comes in adult women's sizes and has shown up in schools) "BOYZ DRULE!" (other half of a slogan that also comes on adult women's t-shirts and has also shown up in schools)

Just so you're aware: narcissistic and self-loathing traits don't cancel each other out. It's not unusual for people to be full of themselves when they're winning but crashing disastrously when their luck runs out. That's the outcome when adults engage in behaviors from both of the two preceding lists.

You discourage both narcissism and self-loathing by consistently engaging in these practices instead:

- Give babies and toddlers plenty of care AND emotional engagement. Respond to them in a friendly way.
- Give kids positive feedback for what they DO: you worked hard on that project! Thank you for helping me with that chore!
- Protect kids from all kinds of abuse inside and outside the home, talk them through their problems, and give them enough warnings about the dark side of life that they have some chance of handling it on their own when you're not around.
- Family fun activities instead of commercial entertainment with its undesirable messaging.
- Keep your kids away from bad influences and bad influences away from your kids.

* The English words "kin" and "kind" are related to each other, and also to the German word "Kind" (child). Your kin-folk are supposed to treat the family Kinder kindly. Then things broke with ham-fisted accommodations to civilization and industrialization.

There's been a lot of discussion about the relative importance of dads for girls versus boys. The stakes are high in both cases. Dads protect daughters from sexual exploitation (often enough sons too). Obviously, girls don't need to learn how to be a man, but they do benefit from learning to relate to a man. Girls who are treated kindly by their fathers have higher expectations of their treatment by other men. Having a loving relationship with a man also helps them resist the misandric messages they'll get from teachers, youth group leaders, women's groups, the media, and commercial entertainment.

As for sons, "It takes a man to raise a man."

Within a week I had moved to a place in the mountains, preparing a room for my child.

Within a fortnight my hired bounty hunter was on the trail, searching for my stolen son.

Six weeks after that terrible night of shock and loss my child ran at last across the courtroom lobby into my arms. I vividly remember hoisting him up and turning away from the audience of court officers and attorneys and special advocates and taking several quick steps away as tears poured out of my eyes.

My little son held my face in his hands and his own was full of happy awe as he brushed the tears away and hugged me tightly, the smile on his face the most beautiful I'd ever seen.

He never left my custody again.

—Ivan Throne, The Stolen Son, *The Nine Laws*

For a while now there has been an epidemic of "lost boys" whose existence was tolerated by his mom and his disengaged or absent dad, but not really valued. They didn't get enough attention from their parents, and in schools and other institutions, they were constantly exposed to the subtext that they're worthless. Their self-esteem and their drive are shot, and they end up with symptoms of chronic depression, often in conjunction with addictions to computer games or pornography, looking for that dopamine hit.

You might be one of them, in which case you wouldn't necessarily realize it because you'd be habituated to it (or in other words, "a fish doesn't notice water"), and you might have managed to become a dad yourself despite your bad start in life. To the extent that you can give your son time, attention, and a father's love, you can protect his self-esteem and at the same time, fill up that hole in your own heart.

Probably the most important thing a father can teach a son is to resist expendability. Sperm is more abundant, and therefor cheaper, than eggs; this fundamental biological fact is at the heart of everything it is to be a man. At this moment in time, especially with so much built-up infrastructure that makes life without a man relatively easy (a situation that won't last forever, by the way), men are almost ubiquitously considered not only expendable, but increasingly, superfluous too. Every man's goal in life should be to resist being expendable by making himself indispensable. Show your son that you value him, and teach him to prepare himself for doing great deeds.

We interrupt this program...

Jason sat in the chair in his pajama bottoms, arm around Kai who was also in pajamas. Herbert was sitting on the other side of Kai in his underwear and a bath-robe.

They were all up early watching Saturday-morning cartoons. Herbert had a non-stop dialog with Kai regarding the action.

Jason was caught by surprise when Vytautas walked into the room. Then he heard Birutė chatting with Veronika in another room.

"I'm just dropping off Birutė," explained Vytautas. He looked nonchalant as if there were nothing unusual about the situation.

Veronika, however, looked somewhere between amused and scandalized when she walked in. "What a fine way to greet our guests!" she scolded, looking at Jason. Apparently it occurred to her that she didn't intend to include Herbert in that assessment. Flustered, she turned to him and added: "You're fine, Sir!" Herbert hadn't been paying attention, looked puzzled at what Veronika had just said, apparently wondering why he was fine, and then returned to his discussion of the cartoons with Kai.

Jason blushed. He hadn't been self-conscious about his appearance until Veronika drew attention to it. Vytautas tried to smooth over the situation. "Sorry, old chap, I shouldn't have wandered in so early in the morning."

Veronika collected Kai, quickly threw some street-clothes on him, then left with Birutė and Kaarina. Jason got one of

Herbert's TV trays, set it up in front of him, then excused himself from Herbert's immediate presence and guided Vytautas into the direction of the kitchenette, which gave him the opportunity to direct attention elsewhere than to his casual appearance. Herbert looked disappointed to be left by himself, but continued watching cartoons.

"Excuse me while I get Herbert his breakfast," said Jason. "Can I get you some too?" Vytautas hesitated to answer, which Jason interpreted to mean he was hungry but reluctant to impose. Jason insisted, and Vytautas gave in.

Jason took a set of molds for making poached eggs off a shelf and set it on the counter. After that, he got some non-stick spray, and then sprayed the molds. Then pulled a container of eggs from the refrigerator, and then broke five of them into the molds. Next, he took a stainless-steel measuring cup, measured out some water, and then poured it into the multi-pot. Finally, he put the molds into the multi-pot, put a lid over the molds to keep the eggs from turning watery, sealed the lid of the multi-pot, and then pushed the buttons to cook the eggs.

As he worked, Jason explained his take on the situation. "She doesn't like it when I let Kai watch television. She's worried it will make him lazy."

"What do you think, Jason?" asked Vytautas.

Jason hesitated before answering. He hadn't considered the matter before. "Well, I suppose that too much television is a bad thing. But it's not like we were going to get anything important done between the time we got up and when it was time for Kai to leave."

"What do you think?" asked Jason after a pause.

"Well, I agree it's not necessary to be busy all the time," answered Vytautas. "And I also agree that too much television is a bad thing. Really bad for young'uns before they can talk."

"Why's that?" asked Jason.

"Because too much of the programming for children involves voice-overs," answered Vytautas. "It makes speech register as noise to children who don't see any lips moving. And the television doesn't respond to their own vocalizations the way a parent hopefully would. Those are contributing factors to speech delays."

That triggered an alarm inside Jason's head. He began searching his memories. He wasn't sure, but it did seem as though most of the offspring of yuppy parents he knew were late talkers.

"Luckily Kai talks just fine, but now I'm concerned about the younger ones," admitted Jason. "And truth be told, Kai is a bit under-motivated. I wonder if she's right that the television is contributing to that."

"Well, look at it this way," said Vytautas. "You get good at doing whatever you practice. If you frequently practice watching television, you get good at that."

Jason chuckled at the thought of being "good at" watching television. Then it occurred to him what Vytautas was getting at. "Which also means that the more you practice watching television, the less time you have to practice anything else."

"Right," said Vytautas. "And there's something else you should be aware of. Imagine your thoughts as you and Kai watch television. OK? Now, think about what your thoughts would be like if you were assembling something like a model ship or a model car. Notice anything different?"

The first thought that occurred in Jason's mind was about the zombie-like state of someone watching television. But that was what it looked like on the outside. What did it feel like on the inside? He gave it some more thought.

He tried to answer Vytautas's question, speaking slowly as he thought out-loud. "Well, when we're watching television, we're just passively responding to whatever is going on in the action. When we're assembling the model, we have to make plans and decisions. We also have to keep comparing our work against what we think it should look like."

"That's the difference between 'passive attention' and 'active attention'," said Vytautas. "Active attention trains the parts of the brain involved in making plans and carrying them out. Passive attention doesn't."

"Active attention doesn't just spontaneously develop at some magical age. Never exercising it is how you get teenagers and adults who can't concentrate on anything, or see a project through to completion."

Something clicked for Jason. But first, he felt the need to make an excuse. "I guess I thought the TV was OK because a lot of it is educational programming."

"Ehh, well, that's the trouble," said Vytautas. "People assume that educational programming is good for kids. But they don't really learn all that much from it, and they're getting way too much.

"It's not just the telly. It's any passive activity. Computer games and social media are particularly bad because they're constantly handing out little rewards, like points or 'likes', which actually kill our drive for more important accomplishments.

"People assume reading is good for kids. Some is good, but too much is too much. Passively listening to the teacher prattle in school isn't training them to actually do anything either. It's just more passive attention."

The multi-pot beeped to indicate the eggs were ready. Jason released the pressure.

"I don't watch all that much TV myself," said Jason sheepishly as he fetched bread for the toast. "Usually just a show or two to relax after work."

"Well, it's true the telly can be relaxing..." started Vytautas. Then, after a hesitation, "...though probably not in a good way."

"What do you mean?" asked Jason as he put slices of bread into a small Japanese toaster-oven and pushed the buttons.

"You realize that television is extremely hypnotic, don't you?" asked Vytautas. "And not in a good way. Dark hypnosis."

Jason stopped working and gave his full attention to Vytautas. "Jason, have you ever decided not to watch television, but gotten drawn in anyway?" Vytautas asked.

Jason grinned good-naturedly and confessed. "Yeah, all the time. Often happens when Kai turns on some show that really is silly, and yet somehow I get distracted by it and end up watching it anyway. So what's up with that?"

"One theory is that the sudden discontinuities when they change cameras are interpreted by our brains similarly to when we spot sudden movement out the corner of our eyes. 'What was that? What was that?' It keeps drawing our attention," answered Vytautas.

"Of course, being story-like in nature also makes it hypnotic," he continued. "Stories in general are hypnotic. Ever gotten drawn into a good book so much you couldn't put it down to sleep for the night?"

Jason grinned. Vytautas continued. "A good story draws your attention by creating expectations and then leaving you waiting for their fulfillment. If you think about it, a typical story starts out as a familiar pattern that is interrupted: 'Little red riding hood went skipping through the forest on her way to Grandma's house....WHEN SUDDENLY, she was confronted by a wolf!'

"The interrupted goal—getting to grandma's house to deliver a basket of food—creates a sort of mental tension as our brains wait for a resolution. A typical story sets up all sorts of obstacles the hero must overcome in order to resolve the tension."

"For example, all the obstacles that Ulysses must overcome to return home in The Odyssey," said Jason.

"Or all the obstacles that Jason had to overcome to obtain the golden fleece," said Vytautas. Jason grinned again.

"Well, so what's the problem then?" Jason asked. "Aren't stories useful? Don't they teach us some sort of moral?"

"They can be useful, but here's the thing: the classic stories we were just talking about taught personal or cultural values," answered Vytautas. "They were invented for the benefit of the family or the tribe. Typically the really old ones are not moralistic, but were still well-intended as survival stories or to set common cultural expectations.

"Nowadays, the story is more likely designed to get you to behave some specific way, or to believe something, for the benefit of a PR agency's client. It's not for your benefit at all."

We interrupt this program...

The toaster oven beeped. Jason put one slice of toast onto each of three plates, and then lightly buttered them.

"But I think there's a bigger problem than that," Vytautas continued. "Television sufficiently fools our brains that when we watch it, our brains process the story almost as if it consisted of real experiences. But they're not real. They're not even realistic.

"It's not just that people have been known to add fictional factoids from television and movies to their database of facts after forgetting the source," he continued. "It's that a lot of our knowledge is generalized and vague, like much of life itself. A lot of situations are too complex for us to process consciously, so we do the best we can with the rules-of-thumb our unconscious minds derive from our database of experiences. Television simulates false life-experience that creates unrealistic expectations of how complex situations will resolve. To give you just a simple example, television characters tend to put each other down almost continuously, to feed the laugh track, and there don't seem to be any consequences of this behavior. Do you think that's realistic?"

Jason pondered briefly. "No. You'd wreck your relationships talking to people like that."

Jason stared off into space for several moments, then he turned to Vytautas and said: "You know, I wonder if that's why sometimes...well...to be honest...I've done some stupid things in my life...and the consequences caught me totally by surprise."

"Could be, and anyway that is exactly the danger," warned Vytautas.

Jason pulled the eggs out of the multi-pot. He put one egg on a piece of toast. Then he got a mug, poured in some hot water from an Asian-style instant hot water pot, and added some instant coffee crystals. It's all Herbert wanted or expected. Jason took the items over to Herbert and set them on his tray. Herbert thanked him, and started eating as he continued watching cartoons.

Jason walked back over to the kitchenette. Now that they were talking about the dangers of television, he remembered a previous conversation on the topic. "You know, now that I think about it, I wonder about something my brother Doug told me once," said Jason as he prepared plates for Vytautas and himself. "He was complaining about the subtexts in children's shows. At the time I assumed they wouldn't put anything bad in kids' shows, so I didn't really pay attention. Now I'm wondering."

"I think I know what he's talking about," said Vytautas.

"Like what?" asked Jason.

Vytautas drew a deep breath. "Just one example. Unmistakable pedophile symbols tattooed all over a sympathetic character in a children's cartoon. Look like the ones depicted in an FBI bulletin that was published by Wikileaks."

Jason felt startled by the answer. In a children's show? "Are you sure? That sounds like one of those moral panic rumors that goes viral."

"You can see for yourself. Look up 'FBI pedophile symbols' on Wikileaks. You'll find an FBI bulletin that was leaked. Look for the 'boylover' symbol. You'll find it tattooed all over a sympathetic character in a children's show produced by one of the world's largest entertainment companies."

Jason was horrified. "Why would they do that?"

"To habituate children to themselves and train them to be sympathetic," answered Vytautas.

Jason considered what Vytautas was saying. It seemed incredible. But in any case, it wouldn't hurt to replace TV time with something more constructive.

"Well, maybe it would make sense to make better use of our time," Jason said as he handed Vytautas one of the plates. "When I was younger, I got all kinds of lessons. Swimming, guitar, science camp, foreign language…"

"Good idea," said Vytautas.

Jason thought some more. "Only trouble is…I can't really afford what my dad could. Maybe one kind of lesson." He paused, and then asked: "What should it be?"

"Well, what's most important?" asked Vytautas.

Jason sighed at first, but then he brightened up after considering the situation from a broader perspective. "I guess my own upbringing was a bit too bourgeois for my own good. Never had to make hard choices; never prepared to fight for survival."

"Then how about martial arts training?" suggested Vytautas.

"Eh? How is that a marketable skill?" asked Jason.

"It's not," answered Vytautas. "Marketable skills tend to be specialized. Anything too general isn't marketable because too common. But you still have to start with more generalized skills before specializing. Martial arts teach a certain amount of physical and mental toughness, and self-esteem."

Jason considered what Vytautas had said. "I feel like I could use some toughness and self-esteem myself."

"Then why not sign both you and him up at the school I'm going to?" suggested Vytautas. "One of the instructors has a parent-child class, mostly dads and sons. You could train together Saturday mornings."

Jason mulled it over in his mind as he prepared a cup of tea for Vytautas. The father-son bonding time sounded appealing, but it also sounded like a big commitment. "Well, let me think about it for a while."

He sighed. "But in any case, I guess we ought to watch less TV."

"Are you serious about cutting back on TV time?" asked Vytautas.

"Sure," answered Jason, "Why do you ask?"

"Have you ever noticed that a lot of good intentions fall by the wayside?" asked Vytautas. "You know, 'I should lose some weight'...'I'd like to save more money'...'I'll try to stop smoking'..."

"Yeah, I've noticed, and I can guess what the problem is: lack of commitment," answered Jason. "People who are committed to a goal don't use wishy-washy language. They use language that expresses resolve." Jason took a bite of his toast.

"You're absolutely right and I'm glad you picked up on that," said Vytautas. "It's hard to create mental images of vaguely-defined goals. Language of commitment helps create better mental images of goals, which in turn increase motivation and resolve. You can increase your success in achieving goals by simply stating your intentions in terms of a rule that's easy to understand and imagine."

Vytautas took a sip of tea.

"One way of expressing an intention in a way that is easier for the brain to process is as an 'if-then' rule," he said. "'If I've had one serving of food, then I'll pay attention to whether I'm actually hungry or not before considering a second. If I've had seconds, then I'll skip dessert.'...'If I see something I want to buy, then I'll write it on a want-list instead of buying it on impulse.'... 'If I get the urge to smoke after dinner, then I'll pop a piece of chewing gum in my mouth and head outside for a walk'".

Jason looked at Vytautas a few seconds.

"What are you thinking?" asked Vytautas.

"That sounds too easy," answered Jason. He took another bite of his breakfast.

"You're right to be skeptical," said Vytautas. "I didn't say it always works, only that having a specific rule works better than a vaguely-defined goal. But as a matter of fact, there's experimental evidence that it helps quite a bit. You're about two or three times more likely to succeed in your goal if you express your plan in terms of specific if-then rules."

Jason was lost in thought for a few moments before swallowing. "That's very interesting," he murmured. Then, hesitating, he continued: "I—ah—do have some goals I'd like to accomplish."

He looked back up at Vytautas and added: "Now, what about when you want someone else to do something? Same thing?"

"If you mean do if-then rules work well for giving orders, yes, they do," answered Vytautas.

"Yeah, that's what I meant," said Jason. "What I was thinking of was that Veronika often gives Kai vague instructions, like 'you need to brush your teeth more often.' If what you're telling me is true, then it would make more sense to say something like 'if you've just finished eating, then go brush your teeth'".

"That's right," said Vytautas. "Parents would get higher compliance with the family rules if they just stated them in a brain-friendly way. Unfortunately what usually happens is that instead of telling their kids what to do, they express their desires in vague terms, or tell their kids what not to do, or even worse, just criticize them for what they predict they'll do wrong."

Jason looked intensely at Vytautas. "It sort of makes sense. But Veronika will be a hard-sell."

"Would it help if I were the one to suggest it? Perhaps after explaining the reasons why using the right words can be so powerful?" asked Vytautas.

"Be my guest," answered Jason. "No harm trying, but I should warn you that if she's skeptical as she often is, she'll give you a hard time. Good-naturedly of course".

"I understand and consider myself forewarned," said Vytautas. "I'll bring it up the next time the opportunity arises."

Review

Television influences behaviors and beliefs in ways you probably wouldn't approve of if you were conscious of the consequences.

Books are more of a mixed-bag, depending on the quality of the thought patterns and emotional reactions of the protagonist. Standards are low for the same reason that trashy novels sell in bigger volumes than great classics. Pay attention to what your kids are reading and think about it in terms of the values it models. Some creepy stuff got pushed on my own family as gifts from activist outsiders trying to influence us. Sometimes it's overt, and sometimes its subtle, like the boy-lover symbol mentioned in the story: if you didn't recognize it, you'd suspect nothing. It's everywhere now. Aside from unwanted sexual messages, I'm also seeing a lot of radical political messages. When in doubt, if it feels off or creepy, reject it.

The addictive nature of computers and cell phones kills drive by handing out frequent rewards for meaningless accomplishments. That goes for you too! This is one of the primary causes of the epidemic of chronic low-level depression and lack of drive common among recent generations of young men, ever since consumer electronics became ubiquitous. Put specific daily limits on electronics use, and reserve one day a week (for people in most western countries, Sunday would be a good candidate) to be free of electronics.

> Use language of commitment both in your own self-talk, and when talking to children about your expectations of them. Use "if-then" language to express rules of behavior. Refer to a specific triggering event: "when(ever) X happens".

The Marshmallow Test

The Stanford marshmallow experiment was a series of studies lead by psychologist Walter Mischel regarding a child's ability to delay their own gratification. They were conducted from the late 1960s through the early 1970s. In these experiments, a child was offered a choice between one small reward provided immediately or two small rewards if they waited for a short period, approximately 15 minutes, during which time the tester left the room and then returned. If the child waited for the second reward, then he or she passed the marshmallow test. The name of the experiment refers to a marshmallow being one of the possible rewards, but sometimes other small treats were used, such as a cookie.

Years later, after the children grew up, their ability, or lack thereof, to defer gratification to get the second treat correlated strongly to their personal competence in many different aspects of their lives, including academics, career, and relationships.

The study is now controversial in academia. One of the problems is that the original experiment was conducted on the island of Trinidad, which has an ethnically diverse population dominated by people of Indian heritage and people of African heritage. Those were the two groups studied and contrasted.

Professor Mischel was curious about complementary stereotypes the two different groups had about each other as being hard-working and studious (or, framed negatively, as lacking the ability to have fun), or carefree and lackadaisical.

He ran his experiment using cheap 1¢ candy as the temptation, and more desirable 10¢ candy as the reward for waiting. The Indians significantly outperformed the Afrocaribbeans in terms of being able to delay gratification.

Professor Mischel wasn't trying to prove anything about innate racial differences, though his intentions wouldn't save him from eventual controversy in later decades when the whole concept of the experiment became controversial and is now taboo and a target for attacks. In fact, what he discovered is of interest to the topic of fatherhood: the difference in outcomes between the two groups narrowed quite a bit after controlling for father absence: father-absence was common in the African-descent group, but occurred only once among the Indian-descent group.

Discovering this correlation didn't endear him any more to post-Modernist academics, who think of fatherhood as being an artificial bourgeois "construct."

Over the years, they've constructed variations of the experiment designed to cast doubt on the conclusions of the experiment. What they've discovered is that if you promise children a treat for waiting, but don't deliver it, children's ability to delay gratification decreases. Well, fancy that; behaviors that are rewarded are repeated, behaviors that are punished (by disappointment) diminish; that's already a well-known phenomenon.

But I don't think it particularly supports the social-welfare interventions that the academics are after; government programs are the parties most likely to disappoint. It's dads who deliver.

It does bring up an important point, though: when you make your kids wait for benefits, deliver the goods. Don't say "later," and then later never happens.

Aside from that important point, engaging with your kids in any sorts of projects that unfold over time, and require some diligence and follow-through to complete, like assembling a model rocket or a car, help contribute to their ability to make plans and see them out to completion. Make sure to follow through to completion; that's the reward.

What they're getting too much of instead right now is a lot of passive-attention activities like watching television or playing computer games. Those activities are often suggested by the parents as virtual baby-sitters, for lack of parental attention.

Kids who are self-directing are more resistant to vice-pushers and other bad influences than passive kids. When something else like a television or computer game, or someone else like a teacher directs all their attention, and they just passively respond to it all, they're more likely to passively respond to a vice-pusher. A kid who already has his or her own plans and a firm commitment to carrying them out can say "no thanks, I've got my own plans."

Trouble

Jason came home to a cold and lonely house. Herbert was in his bedroom, napping, which was probably a good thing; otherwise, he would have been neglected.

It was unseasonably chilly, so Jason turned on a little heat and started searching the kitchen for something to cook for supper. He assumed Veronika would be tired and hungry when she got back and would appreciate having something ready.

He set the table first because the multi-pot cooked fast. He waited until almost the last minute and then started heating it. Once done, supper sat two hours waiting to be served.

Jason was disappointed and getting a little worried. His relief when Veronika showed up at the door was short-lived. Something was wrong.

Nothing too serious, but she was clearly agitated. He wondered if it had anything to do with Angelina's presence at her side. He assumed without asking that she would be spending the night. Jason never had a chance that evening to find out what series of events had lead up to the present situation because Veronika was busy getting her own children fed and off to bed.

It turned out that Angelina had a mild fever. Jason negotiated with her to drink some hot lemonade with honey. Instead, she wanted soda, but when he explained that he didn't have any, and that the hot lemonade would make her feel better, she deigned to accept the offer.

While he was in the kitchen getting it, he was startled to hear the voices of strangers shouting. He recovered quickly after turning his head and realizing that it was the television blaring. Angelina had turned it on without asking. Jason quickly realized that Angelina was acting on an old habit, and that although it might have awoken or even startled Herbert, her intentions weren't malicious.

By now, Angelina was too dispirited to put up a fight. Jason turned off the television, gave her the hot lemonade, put his arm around her, and waited for her to drink it. She started flagging before she finished. Jason put the remainder away, then picked up Angelina, brought her into the family bedroom, and put her down on the bed. He then went and got the cushions from the sofa and some blankets and sheets to make a makeshift bed, which he put her in as soon as it was ready. He tucked her in, stroked her shoulder, and told her she'd probably feel better in the morning. If she didn't, he'd call the doctor's office.

He stayed by her side until she drifted off to sleep, which didn't take long.

The next evening, when the subject came up again after Angelina had been returned to her home and Veronika was in a better mood, it turned out she wasn't angry so much as appalled. He learned the details over dinner. Jason wished he would have gotten the story privately before his family's dirty laundry was aired in public, but the damage was already done, so he swallowed his pride as he listened to the details.

Veronika's theatrical style of recounting it didn't help matters. "We knocked on the door, but there was no answer. We knocked again and no answer. We wondered if they had forgotten about us and had gone out for the day, so I put my ear to the door and listened carefully…"

"WELL, I didn't need to listen so carefully! I soon heard a commotion that Birutė heard too without having her ear on the door! They didn't notice us knocking because their attention was already too distracted by the…" She paused as she thought of the right word in English. "…pandemonium within".

"Once we finally got Barbara's attention, she opened the door for us, but then she couldn't divide it between Angelina and us. Not only that, but the more she tried to talk to us, the more Angelina started acting up."

"More craving for attention", sighed Jason.

"Well, unfortunately, the whole day was a disorganized mess," said Veronika. "Your sister-in-law kept referring to 'their routine', but as far as I could tell, there wasn't any routine." Jason wasn't surprised by her disdain; Veronika was one of the best-organized people he knew. He looked over to Birutė to see her reaction.

Being a respectful person, Birutė appeared reluctant to express her analysis of what happened, but he could tell she had something she thought needed saying. He coaxed her by asking.

"Well," she said hesitantly, "I don't want to sound critical or assume that it's any of my business. I just want to say what I would have done in that situation. First of all, there would be an overall daily routine, including on weekends. Structure helps children know what to expect. When there are special activities, then I would have involved Angelina in the planning for them. That would have made a big difference in her behavior."

"That's exactly it!" exclaimed Veronika, shaking her pointed finger for emphasis. Veronika wasn't shy when she was sure she was right. "Everything revolved around Barbara's plans. Angelina's involvement was more like an afterthought. Like what happened at the supermarket that morning. The girl was obviously bored out of her mind."

"What happened at the supermarket?" asked Jason, curiosity overcoming the dread of finding out.

Veronika looked encouragingly at Birutė to explain. Birutė hesitantly complied. "Well...yes, as Veronika said, she was bored. She kept getting into mischief or demanding treats. Barbara kept saying 'No!', 'Stop it!', 'Cut it out!', 'Quit that!', 'Knock it off!'".

Vytautas looked pained. Veronika and Jason turned to face him and looked at him expectantly. "Well," he said, "it's just that telling children 'no' and 'stop it' isn't much help. Let's assume they actually obey, which, honestly, is a stretch. Then what? Do parents really expect their children to suddenly become inert? Telling them what not to do doesn't fill the void, and nature abhors a vacuum. It works better when you tell your kids what you want them to do. She should have said something more like 'come over and help me pick out some tomatoes.' If for some reason you're not quite as creative as they are in filling in the gaps, then at least be a little more specific about what it is you don't want them to do, which will give you a bit more time to think about what you do want them to do. It's best to give them some options that might not have occurred to them".

"Well, eventually she found something to do," said Birutė. "She slipped away and started playing with the coffee grinding machine. She was quite rough with it, and spilled a lot of coffee beans all over the floor. Then as soon as we were busy trying to pick them up, she pulled a toy from a display and started to open its package, and screamed at us when we took it away. We had a rough time trying to keep her under control. There was a lot of running, screaming, and mishandling of store property. Barbara was clearly embarrassed by all the unwanted attention. It would have been different if Angelina had been involved in the shopping, but she wasn't, not at all."

"Well, shopping for groceries probably really is a boring activity for kids," mused Jason.

"Boredom tends to imply lack of mental engagement," said Vytautas. "You're thinking about what you'd rather be doing than what you're actually doing."

"Well, then how do you mentally engage a child into a shopping excursion?" asked Jason.

"You need to make them aware of the connection between the activity and something they care about—something with emotional attachments. I don't mean it has to be thrilling—it doesn't take much to prevent the boredom. Just making her aware of the connection between shopping and what she's having for dinner would help. Obviously, she cares quite a bit about that!" said Vytautas.

"Yeah, she does, but I have a feeling just informing her of the connection wouldn't work," said Jason.

"That's right," agreed Vytautas, "she needs to perceive it for herself. People care more about their own opinions than they do about other people's. She needs to really think about it for herself and create her own mental models of the connection between shopping and eating, and how shopping will accomplish a goal she has an interest in. The more vividly you paint a picture of the situation for her, the more likely she is to be on-board the plan on her own account. It also helps if you can involve her in the activity as much as possible. She could take items off the shelves as directed, and load them into the shopping cart."

"OK, I understand, but let's say I wanted to run some errands with Kai. How would I 'paint the picture' to get him on board the plans for the day?" asked Jason.

"Just talking about how you were going to plan your day would help. Daily planning with your child is a good habit to get into," answered Birutė. "But if you really want to drill it in, you can rehearse everyday situations so that your children have a sense of what kind of behaviors are expected in those situations. I would organize games where we pretend that we're shopping in a grocery store, or visiting the bank, or participating in church. Part of the game would be to demonstrate the correct behavior."

"That makes sense," said Jason. "I've been thinking how kids are allowed a lot of leeway to horse around on the playground—how are they supposed to realize that the grocery store or for that matter the church are any different, without actually learning?"

"And speaking of learning, that's a process. It takes time," explained Vytautas. "Children can only behave themselves according to the level of self-control they've learned up to that point. Some kids can remain engrossed through an opera and afterwards comment on the quality of the performance. Some can't sit through a ten-minute wait in a doctor's lobby without getting dangerously bored. It's a matter of how much self-control they've built up. It's a lot like physical exercise; you have to build up to it. If a shopping trip is too challenging, start with something easier and get that under control."

"I have a feeling that a lot of parents don't realize what they're missing," said Birutė. "They think of their children as being a nuisance for getting things done, when it would be mutually beneficial for them to be training a helper whose company they happen to enjoy."

"OK," said Jason. "We still haven't gotten to how Angelina ended up at our house."

"Do you want me to skip ahead to that part?" asked Birutė apprehensively.

"No, better hear the whole thing now for a chance at avoiding unpleasant surprises in the future. What happened next?" asked Jason. He had a feeling there were a lot more unpleasant incidents to be disclosed.

Birutė thought about it. "Oh yes, I remember: she helped herself to some donuts and threw them into the shopping cart without asking."

"Well, she DID ask—I mean, after she'd already gotten them," added Veronika.

"It would have been better if she'd have asked before she'd gotten them," Birutė emphasized. "Besides, it wasn't a nice way of asking, was it? She kept asking over and over and over again; just wouldn't take 'no' for an answer...how do you call that?"

"Badgering," Jason suggested helpfully.

"Badgering then," repeated Birutė.

"Trying to wear her mother down by sheer persistence," said Jason. "Birutė, as a professional, how would you handle a situation like that?"

"Well," she said, "it might be reasonable to explain your reason for a decision when you give it, but you only need to say it once. Then if the child doesn't accept your decision, you interrupt the badgering just like you would any other unacceptable behavior. If the child ignores a direct order to drop the subject, you assign consequences for the disobedience."

"So what happened instead?" asked Jason, worried.

"Barbara got very agitated and asked Angelina if she wanted a spanking," Birutė answered.

Vytautas looked pained again. Jason asked him what was on his mind.

"That's still not telling her daughter what she wants her to do; it's a threat disguised as a question," answered Vytautas. "You get a lot less resistance from children when you ask them questions that are easy to say 'yes' to. Do you really expect a child to say 'Yes, mummy, I want a spanking!'? If you feel the need to ask a rhetorical question, how about something more like 'You know the rules. Can I count on you to follow them?' Insofar as it's a command disguised as a question it's still telling them what you want them to do, and it's less confrontational."

"Well, unfortunately, the situation kept getting worse", Birutė resumed. "You know, in a situation like that, a child can barely control her own emotions. A parent who is getting angry is just going to push her over the edge, and that's just what happened. Angelina had a temper tantrum right in the middle of the store, and Barbara lost what was left of her composure.

"That's when Veronika and I decided we needed to take over. It wasn't easy with Veronika having to manage Kaarina too. We took Angelina out of the store, kicking and screaming, as far from other customers as possible, and then just waited until she calmed down."

"Thank you. I appreciate your stepping in like that. So is that how you handle tantrums?" asked Jason.

"That's about as much as you can do at that point," answered Birutė "Preferably, though, you have already talked to them about how to control their emotions while they're still under control. And if parents stay calm, not only are the children less likely to lose their own tempers, but over time they'll learn appropriate emotional responses by copying their parents".

Vytautas nodded. "Unfortunately once they've lost emotional control, not much to be done but try to avoid making it worse. At that point, their emotions are feeding on themselves. That's why it's important to not pour petrol on the flames. Stay calm yourself, and say as little as possible. Be like a brick wall...emotionally non-reactive to the tantrum."

"That's what we did," said Veronika, looking pleased with herself. "Birutė gave me a little signal, and I understood. Other than keeping her out-of-the-way, we didn't react."

"The result?" asked Vytautas.

"Well, she screamed for a few minutes, but the tantrum exhausted itself fairly quickly," answered Veronika.

"As expected," remarked Vytautas. "The whole point of a tantrum is to get a reaction from the audience. If nothing else, they're supposed to feel bad. If there's no reaction, it's not worth the trouble. Like screaming to a brick wall."

Jason sighed. "It's pathetic that a six-year-old would still be throwing temper tantrums. She's not the only one—I've seen a lot of older kids who still throw temper tantrums, as if they were still toddlers. What's up with that, anyway?"

"Oh, you've seen worse than that," Vytautas said. "You've probably seen adults having temper tantrums. Screaming and ranting. Whenever someone is said to 'go postal,' that's basically what's going on: an adult temper tantrum. Being non-reactive—staying quiet and just looking concerned—is also your best bet for an adult tantrum.

"But to answer your question as to why this is happening...well, perhaps it's more a question of what's not happening. You see, humans aren't born with impulse control; we have to learn it. What's not happening is that many of us are not learning impulse control...at least not at the rate that our ancestors did several generations ago."

"Well, if they don't learn it by school age they can get in big trouble," warned Jason. "Many schools have a policy of calling cops on kids having temper tantrums! And if you go postal as an adult, the police are likely to respond with deadly force!".

"Why aren't they learning to control their impulses anymore?" wondered Veronika out loud. "What has changed? What should we be doing differently?"

"The short answer is too many distractions and too much instant gratification in modern life," answered Vytautas. "Sometimes you just have to turn off all the electronics and go play outside."

"Anyway," resumed Birutė, evidently anxious to get the story over with, "after shopping, we had to stop back at the house to put away the groceries. We were almost done when a call came in for Barbara. She took the call while we finished the last few things."

"About two minutes into the conversation, Angelina tried to get Barbara's attention. That didn't go over very well. Barbara snapped at her. Told her 'CAN'T YOU SEE I'M BUSY? LEAVE ME ALONE!'"

Vytautas looked troubled. "That's a message of rejection. That might explain some of Angelina's bids for negative attention. A better message would be to say something like 'I can't talk right now because I'm on the phone. I'll talk to you as soon as I'm done.'"

Birutė continued. "Well, this time Angelina actually obeyed. Left the room, turned on the television, and plopped down on the sofa, angry."

"Yeah, she did the same thing here when she was over last evening," said Jason. "The television seems to be her preferred companion."

"Well, I don't blame her," said Birutė. "Barbara continued chatting on the phone for a long time, happy to continue her conversation in peace. I have a feeling the television keeps Angelina out of mom's way."

Veronika started looking guilty. "Well—I try to give Kai enough attention but—well—with the baby to take care of—and I don't let him watch just anything—I let him watch some educational programs—and a few musicals with songs in them...". She glared at Jason. He let Kai watch pretty much anything. But Jason had learned his lesson and wouldn't do that anymore.

"I know you have a lot to keep you busy," said Birutė. "Maybe Kai could help. He could help you fetch things you need while you're taking care of Kaarina, and help with some of the simpler tasks."

Veronika gave it some thought. "I guess I could involve him more around the house. He's already quiet and lost in his own thoughts much of the time. Maybe it's better not to make him even more withdrawn."

"How old is he now?" asked Birutė. "You know that chores start at three."

"Really?" interrupted Jason, surprised. "What kind of chores do you do at three?"

"Even a three-year-old can put clothes in a hamper, wipe up spills with help, and put toys away," answered Birutė.

"He's four," answered Veronika. "You know, when I was two years old, if something spilled on the floor, my mother would have me help pick it up. I remember helping to pick berries in the garden. It wasn't all that big a deal, but I think that was a good way to get me involved".

"Four-year-olds can make their own beds and help fold simple laundry items like socks and wash-cloths," said Birutė. "It takes time to work with them, but it's worth it in the long run so that you don't end up waiting on teenagers like a servant."

Kai interrupted the conversation to ask for something to drink. Jason got up to get him a few sips of water, then sat down again and looked at Birutė expectantly. Birutė took that as her cue to continue the story. "Veronika and I tried to suggest playing a game to improve Angelina's mood and engage her in a more constructive activity, but she told us 'Shut up; I can't hear the TV'."

Jason blushed. Veronika looked scandalized. Veronika had little patience for mouthy children. Birutė continued:

"Eventually Barbara noticed the time and told her caller she had to get ready for a demonstration at the science museum. Barbara went upstairs for just a few minutes while Veronika and I tried to get Angelina ready. Angelina wouldn't budge until her show was finished. Barbara came down and was livid that Angelina wasn't ready. She said: 'You ALWAYS do this! You knew when we had to be ready by! You're NEVER ready on time!'"

Veronika and Jason turned to Vytautas for another commentary.

He complied. "That's not telling her what to do; that's an accusation. Accusations are assertions you don't want to be true —so—it doesn't make sense to try to convince a child that they are true, does it? Accusations keep attention focused on the problem instead of on the solution. 'Where attention goes, energy flows.' You get more of what you reinforce with your attention.

"By the way, accusations are usually exaggerations. The tell-tale signs are the words 'always' and 'never.' If she ever once were ready on time, then the accusation would have triggered instant disagreement, resentment, and resistance."

Jason looked down, ashamed. Veronika asked him what the matter was.

He sighed. "Brings back bad memories. That sort of reminds me of what happened when my life started falling apart after the divorce. It wasn't so much accusations—though there was some of that too. More like constant criticism.

"Like if I took out the garbage, she didn't say 'thanks,' she complained that I never did it without being told. Then she'd say I forgot to put a new garbage liner in, or asked why I didn't empty the bathroom waste-basket at the same time. If I emptied the dishwasher, she complained that I put some things in the wrong place. If I practiced guitar, she always pointed out my mistakes and said I was bothering the neighbors.

"Eventually it turned into constant criticism. If it wasn't what I did, it's what I didn't do."

Vytautas looked Jason in the eye and said: "I understand why you might feel bad about that. It's discouraging when you do what your parents ask you to do, and instead of giving approval, they criticize. Unfortunately, it's actually rather common."

Veronika nodded. "My mum did that to me too. I'm sure it wasn't anything personal." She tried to sound reassuring, even though she knew the situation wasn't the same. Veronika's mom was fussy but had a warmer relationship with her.

"You get more of what you reward," said Vytautas. "You get less of what you punish. Criticism is punishment for obedience. The child obeyed, but not to the complete satisfaction of the parent. Criticism discourages the child from wanting to cooperate at all. If he does the job—however poorly—and is criticized for it, he's apt to think something like 'Fine! Next time I won't bother to do it at all!'"

"That's the way I felt," confessed Jason. "It just got worse and worse until I couldn't take it anymore. She would come home in a fairly good mood that soured quickly. I got the feeling it was my very presence. So, I left. I thought she'd be sorry because she'd have to do all the chores I was doing herself. But she didn't act sorry at all. Was much happier after she had to do the whole messy job herself, than to have me do any of it at all. It didn't make sense."

"Obviously it wasn't the garbage, or your performance," said Vytautas in a low voice. "It wasn't you, personally. We can talk about it some other time. Don't feel bad about it."

"There's something I still don't understand," said Jason. "I understand what I'm supposed to do to discourage a child from doing something he's not supposed to. But what's the right way to deal with a child who's doing what he's supposed to do, but not very well?" In other words, what could my mom have done to have gotten me to do a better job?" It occurred to Jason that the least he could do was not repeat the mistakes of the past.

"Excellent question. The short answer is you don't punish under-performance, because that's a counter-incentive to perform at all. Instead, you reward performance, but only top performance. Another time I'll give you a fuller answer, but it's a long one, and I don't want to sidetrack the conversation before hearing the rest of Birutė's story."

"Where was I then?" Birutė thought for just a few seconds, and then her eyes lit up. "Oh yes, getting ready to go see the demonstration at the science museum. Well, once we were all ready, we headed out the door and down the street. Now one of the reasons Barbara wanted to go in the first place was because some of her friends would be there as well, with their own children. And on the way to the bus stop, we ran into one of them."

"She had her son with her...," Birutė started, but then she and Veronika suddenly looked at each other and chortled. "...well, we eventually discovered it was a son. What threw us off was that she had him in a flowery pink jumpsuit, with two little braids down the back, and his name is Blythe."

Jason cringed. His wife and Birutė were both still a little naive about that sort of thing. Jason didn't quite understand it himself, but he knew something sinister was going on and didn't' think it was a laughing matter. "That's her friend, Moriah," he said. "She's a teacher in one of the public middle schools. She's kind of weird—and not in an endearingly eccentric way. I'm pretty sure that dressing him as a girl is her idea, not his. She started imposing that on him before he was old enough to express a preference. She and Barbara are part of the same parenting groups."

Jason hesitated before continuing: "She has nothing good to say to me or about me, and to be honest, the feeling is mutual."

"Well, he must love her anyway because she was holding a very expensive lily in her hands," said Birutė. "Several huge open flowers, a few buds, and stem. The stem looked like it had been torn off rather roughly. On the way back home later in the day, we spotted several damaged lilies of the same type, one missing the flowers, in one of the yards we passed. We had already guessed what had happened, because he was still swinging a stick at the flowers in other people's gardens that we passed along the way to the bus-stop".

Jason rolled his eyes. "Let me guess: his mother did nothing to stop him from vandalizing other people's' flowers. Probably didn't apologize to the owner of the lilies either, or pay for them."

"Apparently not," answered Birutė. "When we ran into them, she was ranting about something that had happened at home, but paid no attention to the stick. Then she withdrew attention from him completely once she started talking to Barbara."

Jason shook his head. "I don't understand what it is nowadays. A lot of parents are oblivious to their children's lack of respect for the rights of others."

"I don't entirely understand it myself," confessed Vytautas, "but I do perceive that a false dichotomy between abuse and neglect is the basis for rationalizing a lot of bad parenting choices. Abusive parents rationalize that they're not overly-permissive, and negligent parents rationalize that they're not abusive. Some parents are abusive and negligent; they're not mutually-exclusive at all. The reality is that abuse and neglect are two sides of the same coin".

"Well, we held our tongues about the lily caper, but I don't think Moriah approves of us very much either," huffed Veronika. "She expressed her disapproval when she heard that Kai doesn't go to preschool. She informed me that I was a negligent mother and that he wouldn't be ready for school!"

Vytautas sighed. "It used to be that Kindergarten was considered more than enough to compliance-train them for school, but they keep pushing it earlier and earlier. They tend to see it as remediation for increasingly difficult-to-manage children. However, the preschool teachers are at least as incompetent at maintaining discipline as the parents".

"Then I regret to tell you what happened next," said Birutė. "There was some misbehavior on the bus involving Blythe and one of his pals who got on later. They were being pointedly rude to each other and calling each other names, apparently as some sort of jealous rivalry even though they apparently consider each other friends. But the real mischief was at the museum. It wasn't just the boy and Angelina though; it was their entire group.

"You know the dinosaur exhibit? Well, one boy climbed right into one of the dioramas and began abusing the robotic dinosaur. And in the room devoted to the solar system, several children were using the planets suspended on poles as a jungle-gym. They grabbed onto the bigger planets like Jupiter and Saturn and swung around on them.

"Throughout the museum, they banged on buttons, and, if the display didn't do anything sufficiently interesting, the children just moved on to the next exhibit immediately. They weren't interested in the science. Their expectation seems to have been that they would be entertained, not that they would learn anything."

"Didn't they bring along enough adult supervisors?" asked Jason.

Veronika scowled. "How many are enough? Besides, they were too busy playing with their phones to pay any attention to the children! Birutė and I were the only ones actually supervising!"

"That's an interesting phenomenon," remarked Vytautas. "Modern children—for that matter, even a lot of adults—have relatively short attention spans compared to their ancestors. And you're right, they have unreasonably high expectations of being kept entertained.

"Too much entertainment is one problem, but worse, it's all the wrong kind. It's all the kind that requires passive-attention instead of active. Television. Computer games. Electronic music and video players. Even books. Passive-attention activities make horrible babysitters. Parents make liberal use of them because they keep the child quiet, but they pay in the long run with a child whose attention span and ability to plan his own activities and keep himself on track never develops.

"School is another passive-attention activity. You're expected to be quiet and passively listen to the teacher. The younger kids are getting sent to preschool, the less developed their ability to make their own plans and stick to a goal."

"I understand what you mean, but it's hard for a busy mother to give her own attention to any one child all the time—especially when there are others needing attention!" said Veronika, looking down at her daughter.

"That's precisely why you have to encourage their own ability to plan and self-direct," explained Birutė. "Using the television as a babysitter is compensation for children not having daily routines, not having assigned chores, and not having a habit of initiating their own constructive activities. Years ago children could play for hours with no more supervision than an adult somewhere in the general vicinity.

Older children who have learned to keep themselves occupied only need full attention from time to time."

"That must be so," conceded Veronika. "Families used to be a lot bigger than they are now. One of my grandparents grew up with eight brothers and sisters, and I was under the impression that the generation before that was even bigger. The mother couldn't possibly have divided up her time among so many children, if they weren't taking care of themselves from a young age."

"It sounds like the trip to the science museum was a fiasco," commented Jason. "What happened next?"

"Unfortunately there was more trouble involving Moriah," said Birutė. "We noticed her son reaching into the wiring of one of the displays, and I didn't think that was safe, so I talked to him about it."

She looked troubled as she continued. "His mother started noticing what was going on, and was furious. Came over and expressed her outrage because we were talking to her son about how he was handling the machines."

Jason was appalled. "Cares more about her own fragile ego than his safety or the museum's property. Unfortunately it's not just her. That is so typical of a lot of parents."

Birutė continued hesitantly. "It got worse. On the way back from the science museum, a squabble broke out between Blythe and another boy. That got Moriah's attention. She came over and slapped Blythe hard across the face."

"I'm disgusted but not surprised," said Jason. "I feel sorry for him. By the way, the bumper sticker on her Prius says 'Teach Peace'."

"No, it's not surprising," agreed Vytautas. "People tend to see what they believe, and her bumper sticker tells us what she believes about herself. It sounds like her self-image is fragile, and she reacts too much to what's going on. Needy for approval and easily provoked to anger.

"If you've ever seen any documentaries on situations where the child is totally out of control—you know, the real horror stories—you'll very often notice the primary caregiver having that kind of personality."

"If that would have been Kai, the first thing I would have done is asked each boy what had happened," said Veronika. "You know—sort it out. Resolve the dispute, then talk about ways it could have been avoided in the first place. She didn't care. She just lost her temper over the commotion."

"When adults don't care about children's rights or how they see the situation, that undermines respect for their authority," commented Birutė.

"I don't think I'm anywhere near as emotionally unstable as Moriah is," said Jason, "but I worry that it's just a matter of degree. How are you supposed to stay calm when a child has just done something to upset you?"

"Well, first of all, the child does not upset you," corrected Vytautas. "The child can not reach into your head and push a button to make you angry or upset. You upset yourself.

"Our emotional reactions to events are not conscious choices, so for that reason, sometimes we disown them. If you're tempted to disown responsibility for your emotional reactions, bear in mind that makes you more like Moriah."

Jason grimaced, and then shuddered a little. He was uncomfortable with the thought of thinking or behaving like Moriah.

"Our unconscious minds are programmed to react a given way, and that's the way we're going to react," continued Vytautas. "The good news is that there are ways to change our own pre-programmed behaviors. Our unconscious mind does almost nothing but recognize a pattern, and then respond. If you change the way that you interpret a situation, you'll tend to change the way you respond to it.

"If your beliefs regarding misbehavior involve concepts such as 'being' 'bad,' 'disrespectful,' or 'disobedient,' then you're likely to react with anger."

"Well, now that you mention it," mused Jason, deep in thought, "Moriah does tend to blame other people for her own hostility. So it would make sense that she gets angry when her son doesn't do what she wants. She thinks it's his fault."

"Whereas if she thought of misbehavior in terms of a natural and healthy instinct to seek pleasure and avoid pain, that simply hasn't yet learned to recognize and operate within the boundaries of other people's rights, then she wouldn't get so angry," said Vytautas.

"Something else that helps is confidence that you know how to handle any given situation," he added. "You'll be less likely to get angry if you have alternatives to violence."

"So what happened next?" Jason asked Birutė. Horror had given way to a need to know.

"Well," started Birutė, "after we got home, Barbara intended to let us go for the day, but the phone call she had received earlier was an invitation to dinner and theatre with some of her friends. There hadn't been time to arrange for a babysitter, and I started noticing that Angela was quieter and less active than she had been the rest of the day. That made me suspicious.

"I felt Angela's head and thought it was a bit warm. Veronika felt it too and agreed. So we tried asking for a thermometer, but by that time, Barbara was very distracted trying to get ready for the evening.

"We looked around for Aimée, but she was nowhere to be found." Birutė paused shyly and then found it difficult to continue.

Veronika took over. Jason could guess what was coming next. "As far as we could tell, your brother and sister-in-law were planning to leave a sick child home alone so that they could go out for dinner and theatre with friends!" huffed Veronika indignantly. "Your brother came home, handed Angelina a present, and off they went. I barely had time to inform them in passing that I'd take Angelina with me before they were out the door."

Jason blushed. "I don't know why they make such poor parenting decisions," he muttered. "All I know is Barbara's family life was fairly normal other than her parents always pressured her to succeed. She was always made to feel like her parents' approval was contingent on her having a great career. I don't know if she has ever felt loved, and it's made her a needy for approval. Not so much in a sickly way like Moriah, but I think her need for acceptance has compromised her judgment.

"As for Doug, I know for a fact that he's always wanted to be a good father despite the way we were raised. It's not that he ever had his heart set on having a glamorous career, and it's a good thing, because his isn't. His bosses are constantly brow-beating him. But he doesn't know what else to do than work lots of extra hours to try to placate them, and then he comes home and takes a very passive role in family life. He spoils Angelina with a lot of gifts and treats. Probably to make up for lack of attention."

Vytautas sighed. "It seems as if most modern western cultures put a low value on family and high value on personal gratification and self-image," he said. "Once my family got established in London, priorities changed a lot."

"When we moved away, it wasn't any big deal," Birutė noted sadly. "In fact, we were expected to go wherever our careers take us. Everything seems to revolve around career. The idea is that you have this great career so that you can make lots of money to afford all the toys you need to be happy and prove your value as a person."

She looked down, deep in thought. "Our careers are not so glamorous. I couldn't find anything around London; the market's saturated and it's shrinking as the economy gets worse." She paused, then added wistfully "I see my job as a means to an end, not as an end in itself. I work to support our family that we want to have."

"Well," said Jason, "things should be looking up soon. It sounds like you know what needs to be done to help Barbara and Doug. I assume she made you an offer?"

Birutė looked up suddenly to meet his eyes, then looked down again, blushing. "No," she muttered under her breath. Veronika looked concerned and put a caring hand on her shoulder, and Birutė spat out the verdict: "She said that I did not meet her minimum standards."

Jason exhaled heavily. "What standards?" he asked rhetorically. "I'm sorry about that. It wasn't you. I bet it was Moriah complaining about you. Barbara is easily influenced by her friends' opinions. Besides, they don't have trained nannies; they have maids. They aren't willing to spend the money specifically on their kids. All they want is for an adult to mind the household and do the chores after their kids come home from school."

The phone rang. Jason excused himself from the table to answer it. He picked up the phone, and then said "hello this is Jason" as he went out the door into the back-yard so as not to disturb the conversation.

Veronika was clearing the table when he opened the door to return to his guests and his wife. His eyes met hers as he stood in the doorway.

"I need to leave for the hospital right away," he said.

Review

Language like "stop it!", "cut it out!", and "no!" doesn't re-direct children's attention to better choices, and nature abhors a vacuum. "Stop it" and "cut it out" don't direct their attention anywhere; they'll just tune out those words as noise. If you're having difficulty coming up with the right way to redirect their attention, you could at least tell them specifically what to stop doing. Hopefully, that will give you enough time to think of what they should be doing instead.

"Stop arguing with your sister, and come sit by me." "Put down that stick and come over here."

Remember that you need to displace any activity you want them to stop doing. If what your kids are doing is bothering someone, get them busy doing something else.

Organized routines and schedules help children to know what to expect and what they should be doing. It helps them develop good habits.

Trouble is most likely to happen when children are disengaged from adult activities.

Talking to children about upcoming activities helps the children plan what they will do. Keeping them engaged in the activities is even better.

The amount of time that any given child can spend controlling his or her impulses depends on what the child has built up to. It's like exercise; you can't handle a long-distance marathon if you're totally out of shape. You have to build up to it. Don't expect children to behave themselves during long, boring events unless they've had to chance to build up to it controlling their impulses during shorter events.

A great deal of trouble starts with misdirected attention for lack of attention-training.

Activities in which a child is passively responding to something or someone else, like television, school, computers, electronic games, and even reading, do not exercise planning and self-direction skills that children need to mature. Keep these activities on a strict time budget.

Make time for activities in which children make a plan and carry it through to completion. Imagination games, construction projects, hobbies (television and electronic games are not hobbies), gardening, and chores fit the bill. Budget generous amounts of time for these.

Age-normed peer groups re-enforce immaturity.

Spending time in mixed age groups with adults present, such as in a family and especially so in an extended family, tends to encourage more mature behavior through role modeling and a child's reaction to being watched. Oddly enough, it works both ways: even helping with younger family members can reinforce maturity in older children.

Just spending lots of time around parents tends to improve behavior; there is a "monitor" function in the brain that tells us to behave better when we feel we are being watched. The same phenomenon occurs in adults too which is why employees work more diligently when the boss is around!

Some people are bad influences. They include both children and adults whose patterns of thoughts, emotions, and behaviors are undesirable. Unfortunately, you might have difficulty spotting the red flags because you might be busy at work when they appear. At the first sign of trouble, you need to be ready and willing to pull your child out of the influence of the person you suspect of being a bad influence.

Are your discretionary activities family-friendly? Are you willing to give your own kids your most precious commodity: your time?

> Many fathers give "stuff" instead of time and attention. Give children what they need, and have them earn what they want.
>
> Get out of the habit of criticizing anyone; it's not helpful. Nobody has ever told you "you're right; I screwed up. Thank you for pointing out my mistakes. Now I know better," unless maybe sarcastically.

User-friendly parenting

A parenting stereotype:
Mom: yells at the kids to stop slamming the screen door.
Dad: installs a screen-door closer.

Yet another role for dads that not only did my conservative influencer mentioned in the Preface miss, but for a long time, so did I. I can't find any research to confirm or deny the accuracy of the stereotype; I would hazard a guess it's a taboo question! Whether it's already a general pattern or not, you can make it true of yourself. I know that at our house, it would indeed be typical of me to look for ways to render problems moot. When that's not an option, my next step would typically be to show my kids what I want instead of telling them, or set up reminders that encourage compliance without nagging or yelling. At our house, I'm the problem-solver and peace-keeper.

While looking for answers regarding male versus female parenting styles, I did find polarized opinions regarding whether yelling or nagging is "harmful"; some articles, seemingly aimed at single moms, reassure her that nagging and yelling are OK and normal. Others, clearly aimed either at both parents or at dads alone (some claiming being yelled at by dad more threatening than being yelled at by mom), claim it's harmful. Missing from the conversation was what, precisely, yelling or nagging is being compared to: calmly communicating with kids while maintaining rapport (my choice), or no communication at all (neglect)?

One thing I am sure of just by my own personal observations: nagging backfires. When parents nag, at first the child might comply, but after a while, the constant nagging starts turning into background noise, and they ignore it. The end result is a broken parent-child relationship, and the child becomes eager to find new influencers—often bad ones—who use carrots (typically vices because they're cheap) to motivate instead of sticks.

Yelling brings its own problems: either it escalates to violence, or it doesn't, in which case it too starts turning into background noise that just happens to be at an annoying volume that's hard to ignore, motivating the kids to want to spend more of their time away from you.

Because I don't nag or yell, but instead build rapport, my kids listen to me. They don't always obey, which is why I'm ready to back talk up with non-violent consequences. Fairly quickly, they learn to comply with reasonable instructions, and consequences become few and far between.

Now imagine applying the same strategies whenever you're in a position of leadership: you could be the "good boss" who resolves conflict without creating resentment. Learning how to manage kids teaches you something about managing adults too.

Solidarity

Jason sat alone in the visitor lounge, sometimes looking down, sometimes staring towards the elevator doors. Every time they opened, his heart raced.

Veronika had gone back home to take over from Vytautas and Birutė who had volunteered to stay with the children.

It was 2:38 in the morning when the elevator doors finally opened to reveal the person Jason had been waiting for. Now his heart was pounding so bad it hurt, while his throat was so constricted he wasn't sure he could speak. He launched himself in Doug's direction.

Doug either ignored him, or actually intended to avoid him, as he in turn darted towards the hallway on his right. Jason had to rush to head him off.

Doug shoved him away.

Jason stepped right back in his way. The brothers' eyes locked. Doug looked furious, as if he were about to do something rash...but just grabbed Jason roughly where his arms met his shoulders. Jason in turn grabbed Doug. Doug tried to shove him up against the wall, but despite being stronger than Jason, didn't quite manage it.

"Listen to me. There's no point; she's not there," Jason said.

"Where is she?" demanded Doug. "And where's Angelina?"

The first question seemed odd to Jason. It started occurring to him that Doug's mind was agitated and disoriented. For lack of better ideas, Jason blurted out the facts. "Barbara's down in the morgue. Angelina is at our place. We don't know where Aimée is. Called all over trying to find her".

Doug tried to shove Jason into the wall again. Jason's back just bumped into it. Now pinned by Doug, who half-heartedly tried to shake Jason, then, oddly, pulled himself tight against Jason just before suddenly turning almost limp.

Jason almost lost his balance before realizing what was happening, then pulled Doug back and pushed his head against his own shoulder. He felt the convulsing of Doug's sobs shaking his own frame, and felt Doug's tears against his own cheek.

"Let's go home," Jason said.

"I didn't get a chance to say good-bye," sobbed Doug. He had been incommunicado while trying to make another crisis deadline on his project. The hospital had released Barbara after bandaging up her hand, and the staff never realized how serious her internal injuries were until she collapsed shortly after arriving home. Angelina called 911. Barbara was dead before he ever found out about the freak accident.

Jason didn't know how to respond to Doug's shock and grief, so he decided to change the subject. "Angelina needs you. She's at our home. Come home with me. She'll need your support in the morning."

Angelina wasn't showing any symptoms of emotional trauma that Jason was capable of recognizing, but Jason wasn't sure what to expect down the road. About Doug, he had no doubt that he was not fit to be left alone to his thoughts.

Unfortunately, he wasn't fit to drive either; he was too groggy and incoherent. Jason, on the other hand, never learned how to drive a standard transmission, having had to finish growing up too fast for details like that to have been taken care of. Doug quietly swore at him when he figured out what the problem was.

Jason called a cab. He figured that his brother would be willing and able to reimburse him later, even though it might cost him a lecture about not being able to take care of routine expenses on his own account.

Veronika was an angel. She came out of the bedroom when she heard her husband and brother-in-law enter the house, and quickly made up the hide-a-bed. Then she even set up the cushions from the sofa into a little bed for Jason, so that he could keep vigil by Doug's side. Doug was a wreck.

She told them good-night, gave them each a hug and a kiss, and went back to the bedroom, where all the children were. It was only a 2-bedroom working-man's home, though some of its occupants from generations ago had had surprisingly large families crammed in the same way.

Doug politely kept his voice down but was still grumpy in addition to being distraught. He collapsed into the bed fully clothed. His last words to Jason that morning were "Just shut the ___ up."

Jason settled down on his makeshift bed and wondered at the situation. He felt bad about the accident and its consequences. He couldn't think of anything else he could have done to make the situation any better. Veronika and he had rushed to the hospital. They did their best to comfort Angelina, who herself had a near-brush with death only to be pulled roughly out and see her mother left behind, still trapped in the wreckage. Then later in the day, she was the one who found her mother limp on the floor after hearing an ominous thud.

And Jason was there for Doug, though Doug seemed to be ambivalent to the fact. Jason didn't want to judge harshly, so he considered that Doug was emotionally confused at the moment. Perhaps he'd appreciate Jason later when he came to his senses.

That's when he'd pass along the message that Barbara muttered during one of her last moments of consciousness.

⏳ ⏳ ⏳

The next day was a mess. The first unpleasant surprise was Doug's insistence that he had to get to work.

Jason and Veronika both assumed that grieving after the death of a spouse was a pretty good reason not to show up for work—one almost universally accepted. They were not familiar with the software industry.

Luckily Jason could take a bus to work, so he let Doug borrow the car. Already exhausted, he had to meet Doug at the hospital, so that Doug could rescue his own car from the hospital parking lot, where its parking tab was adding up. On the way, Doug swore at Jason again for not knowing how to drive a manual transmission. Then he told him how disappointed he was that Jason didn't have a career.

Jason wondered why that topic came up, now of all times. It seemed as though Doug would have more pressing matters to worry about. He also wondered why Doug didn't seem to appreciate his help during the crisis. Their dad and their older brother, who both had careers, were nowhere to be seen or heard from.

But he kept his mouth shut. Now of all times, he didn't want to upset his brother by talking back to him—not that he was ever in the habit of doing so.

Doug insisted on going to his own house. Jason reminded him that Angelina was still at his house, but Doug didn't care. Jason mentioned the fact that Aimée had finally been located with one of her mother's relatives—in another state. She left after finding out about the accident. She had no plans to return home.

"I can't do anything about Aimée right now," said Doug. "I need you to take care of Angelina while I take care of personal business. There's insurance that needs to be taken care of, bills, notifying relatives and friends, scheduling a funeral…and I've still got a big project to deliver for work."

"That reminds me," said Jason. "The last time she was conscious, Barbara told me to give you a message. She said…"

"LATER!" barked Doug.

Jason was frustrated, but remained determined to keep his brother from going off the deep end. He could tell that Doug was overwhelmed, even though he remained stubborn and uncooperative. "OK. How about if we stop by your house so you can get some things done, then I will take you back to our place."

"No. I don't want to sleep on your couch, and anyway I need to be home so that I have access to records and my own computer. We'll stay at my place."

Now Jason was bewildered. He wondered what Doug meant by "we." If Doug didn't want to be alone, it seems like he would have been more agreeable to going to Jason's home.

But he felt like he was walking on eggshells as it was, so he agreed and followed Doug home.

Jason made dinner while Doug worked on his computer. Jason served Doug dinner while he continued working. Doug then told him to feed the cat, do the dishes, take out the garbage, and do the laundry.

"Ah, I gotta get up real early in the morning," hinted Jason.

Doug nodded without looking up. Apparently, Jason had his permission to get up early in the morning.

Jason sighed and went to do his assigned chores. The kitchen was a catastrophe, so Jason started on it first, forgetting about the cat until he heard Doug swearing at him from the other room. The cat was demanding dinner from him, and interrupting his work.

Jason came in, picked up the cat, and headed back to the kitchen. He looked around for cat-food. None in the pantry. None in any of the drawers.

He had no idea where people kept cat-food. Now he was worried. Doug would be cross with him if he interrupted to ask where the cat-food was.

He gave the matter some thought, and then remembered that some people serve their cats moist cat-food from a can. He looked in the refrigerator, and found part of an open can. It wasn't enough. He thought some more, and served the cat some half-and-half to keep her quiet.

He'd ask about more cat-food later, when Doug took a break.

Then Jason thought about what he might get yelled at for next, and decided he'd better do the garbage. It would be hard to forget the kitchen, so that could come later.

Then he remembered his mother scolding him for forgetting the recycling. Doug would do the same thing. He looked around furiously for the recycle bin. He found it after a few minutes, hidden behind a slide-out drawer under the counter.

His relief was short-lived. It was getting late, and he still hadn't even started the kitchen. He thought about it, and decided laundry would take a long time because of the need to both wash and dry. He'd better get the wash cycle done, then work on the kitchen for a while, then remember to put the laundry in the drier, then finish the kitchen.

He wondered if he would finish by midnight. "How did I get myself into this plight, how can I get myself out, and how bad is this going to get?," he wondered to himself. So far Doug was frequently cross with him, but still hadn't even so much as doubled up his fist, much less punched him, which is what his last remaining friend Ryan would have done by now. Jason marveled at his brother's emotional self-control.

At two in the morning Doug shuffled in as Jason was putting the last couple of dishes into the dishwasher. Jason felt good about the timing, until Doug said "Look, you didn't clean the counters. Did you do the laundry like I asked?"

Jason then considered that he had forgotten about putting the laundry into the drier. He darted towards the stairs.

"What about the counters? Are you going to leave them like that?!" Doug asked irritably.

Now Jason was thoroughly flustered. It was just like when his mother was constantly irritated with him. He said "sorry" and quickly wiped down the counters, then asked about more cat-food. After taking care of the cat-food, he headed upstairs to the laundry room. Locating it close to the bedrooms and connected to the bathroom had been Barbara's idea.

Doug went into the bathroom to take a quick shower while Jason loaded the laundry into the drier. Jason was standing waiting at the door when Doug came out again. Doug reacted with a smirk.

"Mom and Dad never talked about you before you were born. One day they just brought you home. Up until that point, I hadn't really thought about having a baby brother, but I was so excited. Mom and Dad were already getting up in years not to mention they were so busy, so the first few years of your life you spent a lot of time with me because they were just too tired and busy.

"Mom didn't have enough milk, so when you were bottle-fed, sometimes I did it. I played with you in my room. You slept in a bassinet next to my bed so that Mom and Dad could get some sleep.

"Then one day I entered college and was too busy to spend much time with you anymore. After college I moved out.

"In retrospect, I should have taken you with me and finished raising you. Mom and Dad were really too old and too busy. I think you had every material need but not enough discipline. It was like being raised by grandparents. I would have raised you with a firmer hand".

"You think I didn't get smacked enough?" asked Jason.

"I think you could have used some tough love to build some character and mental toughness," answered Doug. He then playfully smacked Jason on the butt with his towel and told him to take a shower and get to bed.

The shorts were too big. Jason walked into his brother's bedroom holding them up. Doug suddenly chortled at the sight...but Jason noticed some tears streaming down his cheeks. He'd been crying again.

Jason walked up to him and patted him on the shoulder. "You OK?"

Doug nodded but started crying again. Doug told him to close the door and turn out the light. He did so, then he couldn't see his way back. Eventually, he stumbled back, sat back down again, and put his arm around Doug. Doug stabilized his mood enough to talk.

"I keep thinking I'll hear her in the hallway, or she'll step through the door, or I'll see her in some other context I'm used to. Then I remember that I'll never see her again..."

Jason said nothing but just pulled his arm tighter.

"So many threads left untied. I know she knew I loved her. I wish she would have had a better relationship with Angelina".

Jason startled. It reminded him of something. He hoped it would help. "Did you know that Barbara had to kick the window to break it so someone could pull Angelina out?"

Jason felt Doug stir. Then Doug grabbed Jason's hand, pulled it tighter around his own shoulder, and put an arm around Jason. He said nothing.

"Oh, and there's one more thing I need to tell you. Barbara woke up twice. Last thing she said was for me to tell you that your job is in jeopardy, that you should look for another one immediately, and that I should help you whatever way I can."

Doug said nothing. He just continued sitting, for many minutes, until he slowly started slumping over as he fell asleep. Jason assumed Barbara's message must mean something to him, but whatever it was, he apparently had no intention of sharing it with Jason.

For his part, Jason found it difficult to fall asleep despite desperately needing it. Jason had some sense that a trend continues until it exhausts itself. In his mind, he extrapolated the decay that he was beginning to sense had set into his family.

His great-grandparents were reputedly fairly devoted parents. Then his grandparents somewhat looked down on their parents for being "backwards immigrants", and rejected a lot of their values and ways. His parents, in turn, looked down on their parents for not being college educated, and rejected a lot of their values and ways. By now Jason was painfully aware that they put lifestyle choices at a higher priority than their children.

Todd had put off having a family, then married a dubious prospect for a mother. Doug seemed to love his daughters...but Jason had a sense that something was still missing.

Jason knew that Barbara criticized Doug for not taking care of disciplinary issues. He did play with his daughters, and he financially provided for them, but truth be told, being higher up in the corporate hierarchy, Barbara out-earned him. His contribution to the family budget didn't earn him any respect, and his personal status was well below Barbara's.

Something seemed imbalanced. Then it started to dawn on him: in earlier generations, like his grandparents or especially his great-grandparents, dads had more specific roles. The modern trend was for androgynous parenting, but the importance of their roles wasn't equally divided between the parents. Instead, it was mom, and junior-assistant-undersecretary mom. Nor was Jason convinced that trying to balance androgynous parenting was any improvement over the status quo.

The more he thought about it, the more he realized that from generation to generation, the men in his family were becoming increasingly marginal within the family structure. He began to wonder if this was the phenomenon had contributed to the demise of his parents' marriage. He thought about how quick Todd was to placate his unreasonably angry bride at the wedding. Then there was Barbara's friend, Moriah, who didn't have a husband and claimed they were superfluous in the family structure. She had a poster in her class-room with several depictions of various living arrangements, all of them fatherless, with the caption "Families come in all shapes and sizes."

He considered Doug's situation. As bossy as he was with Jason, within his own family he was a somewhat superfluous appendage, or at least, he was treated that way. Barbara had made her plans for the girls pretty much without his consultation. Birthday parties and other special events routinely occurred without his knowledge or presence. He brought home income, but if Barbara had decided to put her personal freedom ahead of his contribution to the family income, she could have traded a modest reduction in her standard of living for it. Many women would have jumped at the bargain. To her credit, she hadn't.

Jason felt uncomfortable judging other people, but it was becoming increasingly clear that Barbara had been somewhat incompetent as a mother. That wasn't her intention, but it was the fact of the matter. To her credit, she had tolerated Doug better than any of her friends would have. She was a better wife than a mother. Most of her friends who had ever bothered to marry were divorcées by now, and not shy about flaunting their personal freedom and encouraging their friends to assert their own.

Jason had a sense that while Doug had never asked to be put down by his wife's narcissistic friends, neither had he ever done anything about it. Of course, just like Barbara had never learned how to be a competent mother, Doug had never learned how to take charge of a situation; instead, he just kept continuing to accommodate, appease, and cede his rights and responsibilities as father, husband, and man.

Jason considered his own situation. Hadn't he, too, been too quick to blame circumstances instead of doing something about them? Wasn't the status quo eating away at Veronika's confidence in him as a father, husband, and man?

🕐 🕐 🕐

Jason felt tired by the time he made it back to Doug's house after work. Doug wasn't back yet, so Jason checked on the cat, worked on some more laundry, and started supper.

Doug got home what for him was early, and sat down to the hot meal that was waiting for him.

"Thanks," he muttered without much emphasis.

Jason sat down next to him at the table. Doug ignored him until he had finished his meal. Then his attention broadened slightly, and he turned to face Jason, who had been waiting attentively for this moment.

"I know that you're under a lot of stress right now. The least I can do is help out. There's not much I can do about Aimée but at least I can help with Angelina."

"How can you help? You've just got Kai and Kaarina and they're both easy. What makes you think you know how to raise a defiant child?" asked Doug incredulously.

"Well, maybe I don't, but Angelina needs to be raised by family, not hired strangers," answered Jason resolutely.

He waited for a response and got none. But he correctly interpreted that to mean he had Doug's permission to take charge of Angelina, so he continued. "As you know, we have Kaarina and Kai to take care of. Kaarina takes a lot of Veronika's attention, and none of us want Angelina to be neglected as a result—"

"She can play with Kai," interrupted Doug. He was trying to be helpful.

"You're right, she can," agreed Jason. "And both of them will need some adult attention and supervision. I suggest that you hire Birutė to take care of them while I'm at work to make sure that she's getting enough adult attention and supervision."

"Barbara said that Birutė is unqualified," said Doug flatly.

"Yes, I heard about that," said Jason. "Do you know what criteria she used to come to that conclusion?"

The question was probably pushing the limits of Doug's involvement with mundane parenting issues, but he did have a sharp memory. He paused to recall her offhand comments. "She said Birutė doesn't seem to know anything about Hightower's theories of child development, or the new affirmative parenting methods." He thought some more. "She also mentioned that she upset Moriah."

Jason looked back at Doug for several tense moments without talking. For the first time in his life, he was going to stand firm with—or perhaps more accurately, for—his brother. "So those were Barbara's reasons. What do you think, brother? Do you think that Hightower, affirmative parenting, or Moriah have been particularly helpful up to now in bringing up Angelina?" he asked.

Doug looked back for a moment, then drifted into thought. He muttered distractedly that he had no idea who or what Hightower was, or what "affirmative parenting" meant. Unlike Barbara, who had been in denial about it despite the constant chaos, he actually had some sense that his daughter's behavior was a problem. Finally, he said: "I guess I don't really care about upsetting Moriah. She doesn't like me either."

Jason interpreted his brother's comment to mean he'd let Jason hire Birutė and he'd pay the bill. Jason exhaled relief as quietly as he could.

"OK, good," said Jason. "Birutė can help Angela work through losing her mother. I've been worried about her not getting enough attention and moral support."

"Well, you know what they say: kids are resilient," said Doug.

Since the problem was already addressed, Jason didn't argue. But he couldn't help wondering who said that and how it could possibly apply so broadly. He didn't think Angelina would fall apart, but she already had a lot of anger, frustration, and hunger for attention. What other feelings she would nurse if her emotional needs continued to be ignored? He considered how angry and alienated Aimée was.

Jason had confidence that Birutė would be a positive influence on Angelina. He wondered what could be done for Doug. He knew that his brother rarely expressed his emotions and never talked about them.

"It hurts me to see that you have so much weighing on your heart and mind," said Jason. His throat felt constricted and his heart was pounding. "I want to help as much as I can. Because you're my brother and I love you." It was the hardest thing he had ever said in his life, and he had no idea why it should be so. His eyes met Doug's.

Doug's expression did not change in the slightest. He just continued looking back at Jason with his usual aggressive stare-down. Instead of feeling relieved to get the words out, Jason was left feeling empty and numb.

Review

A fish doesn't notice water. When family members aren't relating to each other the right way, it might be hard for them to realize that there is a problem, understand what it is, and know how to improve the situation.

The younger a child is, the fewer reference experiences he or she has by which to judge his or her experiences. So a child's external response to a traumatic event might not seem like much, yet it is precisely because their minds are still developing that their experiences have more impact on them than they would if the same sort of event happened later in life. When children have life-changing experiences, like the death of a parent, or their parents divorcing, taking the initiative to provide emotional support helps avoid trouble later. Don't know what to say? Often words matter less than good rapport, managing your own mood, and hugs.

Your relationships can be poisoned by people in positions of influence who don't like you. It's hard for most men to spot, because it happens unconsciously and often behind our backs. As a result, Doug has no idea that Moriah and other influencers have been poisoning his relationships with his wife and daughters for years.

Parenting is often taken to be an unskilled activity that anybody can master without any preparation, so many parents simply refuse to believe that there could possibly be anything wrong with their parenting habits.

Good parenting is a matter of complex patterns of unconscious habits. It's where your attention goes, and how you react to what children do in terms of your emotion, frame of mind, and behavior.

Good parenting is not information. It's also not a course you take in college or in a book you read on child-development, none of which is relevant anyway.

Words & Feelings

"Consider for a moment any one of numerous incidents of purely verbal bullying that have resulted in teenage suicides."

Vytautas paused dramatically to let his words sink in. He was sitting at the dinner table that had been set up in the day-room of the cramped fisherman's cottage. Dinner was over. Veronika had invited him and Birutė over so that he could deliver the promised explanation regarding how it was possible that just a parent's choice of words could make a big difference in how well children behaved. She left a fresh pot of coffee and another of green tea on the table. Kai had been excused to play in the bedroom; Jason held Kaarina on his lap as she quietly observed; and Herbert had retired to his room to read in bed before going to sleep.

Vytautas resumed. "In several cases, the bullies had explicitly stated an intention of goading their victims into suicide, and they were successful, using nothing more than the power of their words.

"With malicious intentions, words can harm. With benevolent intentions, they can heal."

Vytautas poured himself a cup of tea.

"How is it that words can have such power? Consider the story of Pavlov and his dogs. The Russian scientist Ivan Pavlov used to ring a bell whenever he fed his dogs. He found that once the dogs unconsciously learned to associate the sound of the bell to being fed, he could ring the bell, and then the dogs would start salivating, even without offering any food.

Vytautas took a sip from his cup before continuing.

"What happens is that as we learn words, we associate them to the ideas and emotions that we experienced when we heard them. We reinforce those associations with our own memories and our own little stories we tell ourselves to summarize our memories. Let's try an experiment:

"I'd like you to recall an incident when someone mistreated you," he said in a soft, smooth, silky voice. He paused for a few moments, waiting to see signs that his audience had a memory in mind, before continuing. "Treated disrespectfully by someone whose very presence just makes you squirm with unease. Now just imagine that same person ridiculing you with a nasty joke about you, and people that you thought were your friends stand around you laughing, and you realize that they're laughing at you as you feel the blood rushing to your cheeks as the humiliation sets in, you look in their faces and see derision untempered by the slightest bit of pity, and just think about how you'd feel being treated like that…"

It wasn't hard for Jason to imagine; he'd had plenty of humiliating experiences in his life, especially after his parents' divorce. Most of his friends had abandoned him, and a few actually turned on him. It was an unpleasant recollection.

"OK, take a deep breath, snap out of it, back to the here and now…" said Vytautas after a pause.

"Most people who hear words like that will have at least had some unpleasant thoughts or feelings, and a few people might even have been propelled into a bad mood or re-experienced an unpleasant memory," continued Vytautas. "Even people who are emotionally detached from their imagination would probably experience rage or shame if the situation I described happened to them in real life. But the whole experience, just now, and also in the past, was nothing but words."

Vytautas took another sip from his cup.

"Just using their words, parents can trigger the emotions that motivate changes in behavior," he continued. "In fact, they're already doing just that, but unknowingly and typically the wrong emotions and the wrong behaviors."

"Could you give an example?" asked Veronika. "I mean, of things that parents say that encourage the wrong kind of behavior." Jason sensed concern in her voice.

"Yes, of course," answered Vytautas. "One fairly common way of reinforcing misbehavior is to convince a child that there are no alternatives. For example, name-calling."

"You mean like calling a child a 'liar' or a 'brat'?" asked Veronika.

"That's right," confirmed Vytautas. "That's not telling your kids what to do; that's disparaging their character.

"A liar lies—that's what liars do. But a little boy who lied once has the option to tell the truth the next time. Instead of trying to convince him that he'll keep telling lies, simply say to him 'Now tell me the truth'."

Veronika nodded. "That makes sense."

"More generally, it's undesirable to label a child at all," said Vytautas. "Don't tell him he is 'bad' or 'naughty'. Describe what he did, not him personally. You want to focus attention on his behavior, not on him.

"There's another problem with shaming words like 'bad' and 'naughty.' Let's say that a child did something to cause harm to another child. Perhaps yanked away a favorite possession, handled it roughly, and broke it.

"Imagine that he feels ashamed for what he did. Where is his attention?" asked Vytautas.

Three pairs of eyebrows furrowed in thought. Jason was the first to be brave enough to attempt an answer: "On his own feelings?"

"Yes, exactly. But where should his attention be?" asked Vytautas.

"On the other child's feelings!" exclaimed Veronika.

"Quite right," confirmed Vytautas. "Shame can motivate us to improve our behavior, so it's not necessarily a bad thing, but it makes us no more sympathetic to the rights and feelings of others than we were before.

"Most people's sense of morality is based on..."; Vytautas paused dramatically, then added "...fear. Fear of getting caught and punished. Fear of loss of reputation.

"Fear has been the primary deterrent to misbehavior since the dawn of human existence. But there is something better than just avoiding punishment, and that is to act out of respect and empathy for others.

"Someone who makes choices based on fear of punishment might be tempted to violate the rights of others whenever he sees an opportunity to profit with little chance of being held accountable. That's what causes moral breakdowns when nobody's looking.

"Of course, those at the top of power structures aren't accountable to anyone else in the first place. That's what causes tyranny.

"And then there are all the moral catastrophes that happen when, out of fear, other people go along with tyrants. What fear-inducing punishments teach, at some unconscious level, is that 'might makes right.'"

Vytautas took another drink from his cup. "Something else that goes horribly wrong is when shame motivates denial instead of better behavior. Shame can motivate people to look for excuses for their bad behaviors, or to hide them behind elaborate pretexts, or blame them on someone else. That's how you get people like Barbara's friend Moriah."

Jason shuddered at the thought.

"It's not just Moriah," Vytautas continued. "We're all a little like that; it's only a matter of degree. We often think of ourselves as decent people when really all that's keeping us out of mischief most of the time is fear.

"Small children, as well as morally-immature adults, tend to make moral decisions in terms of rewards and punishments," Vytautas continued. "People whom we tend to think of as being at a higher level of consciousness—saints, philanthropists, and philosophers—tend to think about moral problems in terms of the perspectives and rights of everyone involved in a situation.

"So, for example, a four year old might say that you'd better not steal from a shop-keeper because you'd have to go to jail, whereas someone with a more mature sense of right-and-wrong would say that you'd better not steal because theft would harm the shop-keeper and the customers that the cost of the loss is passed on to.

Kaarina was tugging on Jason's mustache. He laughed. But he worried she might be getting bored and wanting more attention. Her grip on his mustache loosened as she yawned.

"There is also the practical matter that fear of stepping out of line hinders people from realizing unconventional possibilities and solutions that harm no-one," continued Vytautas. "It's a common problem in excessively authoritarian cultures, where conformity is given a higher priority than innovation. People are afraid to step out of their conceptual boxes, because they tend to see the world in terms of what they've been told to do, instead of taking initiative and coming up with new solutions.

"So, when you reprimand a child for harming someone else, it's better to direct the child's attention to how the other person feels about being harmed, than to instill feelings of fear and shame for disobedience."

"Well, if the child felt more concern for the rights and feelings of others, he would be less likely to cause trouble in the first place," reasoned Veronika.

Jason noticed that Kaarina had gotten awfully quiet. He looked down at her and saw that she was dropping off to sleep. Veronika took her and excused herself to go put her to bed. Birutė reflexively got up and followed behind to be ready to help out if needed.

Jason thought that was probably the end of the conversation, but Veronika surprised him by seeming eager to resume it after she and Birutė returned. "Earlier you said calling names was one way to reinforce wrong behaviors. Are there others?" she asked

Vytautas.

"Oh yes," he answered. "Even more common than calling names is to make accusations. Remember telling me about Barbara accusing Angelina of NEVER being ready on time? If ever Angelina were ready on time just once, then it undermined Barbara's credibility. And to the extent that Angelina ever internalized it at some level, the message reinforced not being ready on time."

"A similar way is to ask for reasons for misbehavior. Saying things like 'Why don't you finish your homework on time?' or "Why do I always have to remind you to take out the garbage?'."

"That's not telling your kids what you want them to do; that's just an accusation disguised as a question. Consider carefully if it really makes sense to ask questions that you probably don't really want an answer to. That's just going to make them defensive."

"So what kinds of things should parents say to children?" asked Veronika.

"Well, above all, you give them feedback," answered Vytautas. "In fact, for all intents and purposes, effective child discipline is largely a matter of interrupting misbehavior and giving appropriate feedback. Depending on the situation, the feedback is an order, a reprimand, or consequences. In the case of giving feedback for desirable behaviors, it's praise and rewards.

"Drop the pitch of your voice to give an order: 'Use your indoor voice in the house please,'" he said in a deep voice.

"Raise the pitch of your voice to issue praise: 'Thank you! I really like how you help me with your baby sister!'," he said in a higher-pitched tone.

"It's a little like recognizing that the red light and buzzer means mistake and green light and chime means good work," he continued. "It's actually a little nicer and more effective than that though, because instead of giving him an error message telling the child that he did wrong, most of the time we're telling him what he needs to do to do right. It's an encouraging experience for him instead of a frustrating one.

"I once heard a story about the motivational value of positive feedback versus negative. Someone was given a task but wasn't told what it was. He was just told to respond to the audience. Every time he did something that didn't get him closer to the task, the audience booed and hissed. The task was to take a pitcher of water and pour some of it out into a glass. But he became frustrated quickly and gave up before completing it.

"The next person was given a similar task of opening a book and turning a page. This time, the feedback was in the form of clapping and cheering whenever she got closer to performing the task. She completed the task fairly quickly. The reason is because the motivation did not cause her frustration or other negative feelings.

Veronika looked anxious. Now it was time to get Kai ready for bed. Vytautas smiled and said that they could continue the conversation another time. Birutė followed her to the bedroom where they collected Kai.

Jason and Vytautas chatted a few minutes about their work, and then Jason got up to clear the table and start the dishes. Vytautas helped.

They were just finishing when Veronika and Birutė returned. Veronika looked pleased that the boys had cleaned up after supper. She responded by refilling the tea and coffee pots, and then setting out some raspberry and almond cookies that were essentially miniature Linzertorten. Neither Vytautas nor Birutė had the heart to refuse, so the conversation started up again. Veronika encouraged Vytautas to continue telling her about the power of words to manage children.

"Well, you have to choose the right words, and one thing that doesn't work is to try reasoning, especially with younger children," he said. "But oddly enough there is a case where the language of logic is useful to make a connection between behavior and consequences.

"'You need to go sit in the corner because you yelled at me after I told you to stop.'" he said in a serious "papa bear" voice.

"Of course, there's not really any logical connection between yelling and sitting in the corner, but these kinds of sentences help children associate forbidden behaviors and warnings with consequences. You're talking about a behavior and a consequence in a single sentence, causing them both to get recalled and linked in their minds.

"There is another type of language pattern that's useful for giving children information they might not be receptive to," said Vytautas. "The pattern is that you link the information that children might not want to hear, to a statement that they're likely to agree with.

"'I don't want to sit in the corner!'

'Yes, I know you don't want to sit in the corner, and you can go play again as soon as your time-out is over.'"

"Do you think that being agreeable is enough to avoid an argument?" asked Veronika skeptically.

"Not always," confessed Vytautas, "but at least we're minimizing conflict instead of maximizing it. Get into the habit of saying things that are agreeable and respectful of the child's point-of-view.

"'I don't want to go to bed!'

"'I understand that you want to stay up to watch that television show. When I was your age, I too wanted to stay up and watch television, but I had to go to bed on time. I wonder if you've thought about how hard it will be to get up early in the morning for school if you don't go to bed right now?'" Vytautas dropped the pitch of his voice while issuing the command to "go to bed right now."

"What if the child doesn't go to bed after being told?" asked Veronika.

"It's probably superfluous to send him to the corner first," answered Vytautas. "Just pick him up and carry him to bed. The kind of gentle force you use with children does not include slapping, hitting, throwing punches, or shaking. It also doesn't include shouting or any kind of verbal abuse.

"Many parents can physically but gently handle a child only while they are fairly young. For that reason, you want to promptly move past the need to do so. If for whatever reason you are still dealing with violent temper tantrums past the toddler years, well there are ways to do it, but it gets a lot harder.

Vytautas reached for a cookie from the tray, and then took a bite. During the brief pause in the conversation, Jason wondered how hard it would be to set Angelina straight now that her misbehavior had set in for so long.

"Recall that you don't talk too much when giving an order because you don't want to distract the child," resumed Vytautas. "There will be other situations when more talking is appropriate. For example, after the consequences are over, and the child is in a calm and remorseful mood, it might make sense to talk about what happened, and how the situation could have turned out better.

"There will also be times when you didn't find out about bad choices until after the fact, and the case has gotten a little cold to assign consequences. In that case, a reprimand is in order.

"Have you ever noticed how many parents are prone to really tearing into their children when reprimanding them? Instead of telling them what they should have done, they criticize what they did do and stay focused on that. It might sound something like the following..." At that point, Vytautas adopted the manner of an indignant, scolding parent, saying

"I can't believe you lied to me about where you were this afternoon. I am sick of all your confounded lies! One of these days you're going to be sorry when you tell me something, and I don't believe you because you're such a big fat liar. Do you have any idea how much harder my life is because I can't trust you? You don't even care, do you? You are so inconsiderate. All you do is think about having a good time for yourself and then when it comes time to pay the piper you lie about it and think you're not going to get caught. Well, I've got news for you: I am not as stupid as you think. And I'm not going to put up with you anymore...

"And that's just for starts. People can rant like that for a long time when they're angry."

Veronika nodded knowingly.

"What do you suppose is the effect of that kind of rant?" Vytautas asked.

"Probably depends on the kid, and how often it happens," answered Jason. "Might make the kid feel bad. But if it happens too often, they just tune it out."

"Neither of which gets any closer to a solution," said Vytautas. "It keeps attention focused on the problem, and even suggests that the problem will persist.

Vytautas finished his cookie with the next bite, poured himself some tea, and took a sip before continuing.

"There's actually a good reason to bring up what went wrong, so that a child regrets the consequences of his choices. But then you move promptly on to the solution.

"Here is a strategy for administering a reprimand:

"Look them in the eye. For small children, get down on their level.

"Give them your full attention, and get theirs.

"Talk about what the child did.

"Talk about the consequences, preferably in terms that have emotional impact for the child.

"If you have to criticize something, criticize the behavior not the child.

"Start the discussion with the problem but move it promptly to the solution. Depending on the situation, you might need to unilaterally decide on what the solution is, or it might be appropriate to open up a dialog and ask the child to help come up with a solution.

"Tell them what to do, not what not to do, and make sure the rule is expressed in a simple 'if-then' formula, such as 'If you want to go out with your friends, then you have to ask permission first.'

"Solicit a sincere commitment to the solution.

"Now, here is why it's important to get a commitment: it's a strange fact that people often lie about something they did, but less often about their intentions for the future.

"So, for example, if someone tells you that he'll meet you at 12 noon for lunch, he probably at least intends to do just that and if he doesn't follow through, it means he probably forgot or got tied up with something else. After he shows up late, he might fabricate an excuse to save face, but it wasn't his intention to deceive up-front.

"With most people, adult or child, if you're having difficulty getting a clear, decisive 'yes' when you ask for a commitment to the solution, that's a dead giveaway that you're getting resistance and you've still got a problem. In that case, you might have to fish around for what the obstacle to compliance is, but at least you're getting closer to a solution.

"If you get a firm, clear 'yes', that usually means that the child at least intends to comply. He might forget, or allow a bad habit to get the better of him, but at least you've got his intentions on your side.

"If a child intends to comply but has difficulty remembering, think of ways to help remind him without your personal involvement, and make sure that the rule is stated in a clear-cut fashion. If you tell your children to put more effort into their homework, that is too vague of a rule to comply with. If you tell them they have to finish it before playing on their computer, that's a little better, the problem being that it's still missing a standard for what constitutes 'finishing' it. If the rule involves a check for compliance and consequences for non-compliance, that's even better.

"So when you reprimand a child, you might say something like: 'I understand why you would want to meet up at the shopping mall with your friends. Everybody likes to have a good time with people they enjoy. There are times and places where it is appropriate, but there are also situations where it is not appropriate.

"'I asked you where you were this afternoon, and you told me that you went straight home after school. I've discovered evidence that you were not home until after dark. So first you were somewhere you should not have been, and then when asked about it, you lied. That area can get rough after dark, I was left worrying about where you were, and your homework didn't get done.

"'There are better times and places to have a good time with your friends. I've arranged for some events in the past. If you have suggestions for future events you're welcome to suggest them to me. Now I ask you, can I count on you to come home straight after school and finish your homework before 9 o'clock unless we've previously discussed and agreed on a different plan for that day only?', and then wait for a firm commitment to comply."

Jason nodded his head and grabbed a cookie.

"Now there have probably been times you've tried to use words to influence other people, and have failed," continued Vytautas. "In that case, it might seem as if the words were powerless."

"Oh, no, they were powerful, all right!" said Jason, setting down his cookie without having taken a bite. "Either the target turned all the more stubborn, or worse, did exactly the opposite of what I proposed!"

"Well, there's some art to how you use words," said Vytautas.

"Are you sure the problem wasn't with who was speaking them?" asked Jason. "Credibility is a function of status. I have none."

"You're right, credibility is a function of status, but that's unlikely to be an issue with small children as long as you don't cede your authority as father," said Vytautas.

"Then what is the issue?" asked Jason.

"One possibility is if there's no emotional incentive," answered Vytautas. "If you tell your kids to clean up the living room because your friend is coming over, that might sound like a good reason to you but not to them.

"Another possibility is lack of positive rapport.

"There are some people whose opinions you just don't care about," continued Vytautas. "You have no emotional investment in them, positive or negative. You're not even curious about what they have to say, and you aren't interested in committing time or attention to them. This situation is a lack of rapport.

"Now think about someone you don't like. Oddly enough, you are likely to react strongly to things that person says, but it will be in a negative way. You won't believe what they say, and you'll resist doing anything they tell you to do, maybe even do the opposite."

Veronika looked thoughtful. "Hmm. Even people we don't like can manipulate us."

"That's right," agreed Vytautas. "Negative rapport has as much power as positive rapport. That's why some people actually crave it, and end up with a lot of contentious relationships. They'd rather get into an argument than be ignored! The power of negative rapport is probably the main reason that children sometimes taunt or otherwise show blatant disrespect to their parents, and that's why when disciplining your children, you emotionally disengage from the situation, and, if necessary, disengage from the child too to take away the perverse reward of negative attention. So if you send your child to the corner and hear a taunt yelled back, ignore it at least for the moment. Do not allow the child to control your actions, even in a negative way."

Jason nodded. He was beginning to see a pattern emerging.

"Now think about someone you like," continued Vytautas. "When that person says something, you probably listen to and respect what he or she is saying even if you don't necessarily agree with it."

There were nods around the table.

"That's positive rapport," continued Vytautas. "Positive rapport is how you get children to listen to you. It's often enough to motivate good behavior all by itself. Many people remember behaving better for their grandparents than they did for their parents, and one reason is that grandparents often have better rapport with children than parents do.

"Good rapport is built from words and attitudes such as...
'I'm on your side.'
'I hear what you're saying.'
'I'm happy when you're happy. I'm sad when you're sad.'
'I'm a lot like you.'
'We're a team.'
'Yeah, I know what you mean.'
'Really? That's just what I was thinking too!'"

There were nods around the table, and a grin from Veronika. "Well, yes, I behaved better for Oma than for Mama. But, well, Mama frequently wanted me out of the way so she could get work done, whereas Oma kept me busy. Oma had me help her make the beds in the morning, and she had me help in the kitchen. And we did a lot of fun things together too. Oh, and Opa used to take us through his garden, visiting each plant, and he'd pick papayas and guavas and macadamia nuts, and we'd eat some right in the garden, and take the rest back to Oma."

"Your grandparents not only maintained rapport, but kept you engaged as well, wouldn't you say?" asked Vytautas.

Veronika nodded.

Jason felt uncomfortable. Vytautas must have noticed. He turned in his direction, and Jason took the opportunity to get something off his chest: "Veronika's family is more family-oriented than mine," he confessed ruefully. "The adults in my family tend to spend a lot of time in activities that are not particularly child-friendly.

"In my parents' generation, everything seems to revolve around partying with their childless friends. With my dad it's the university scene. With my mom, it's the executive yacht set.

"I think my brothers want to be good dads, but the lives of Doug and Barbara revolved mostly around career, and even their socializing tended to be adult-oriented nights out with associates they thought could help their careers. To her credit, Barbara did pointedly engage in some child-centered activities, although..." Jason's voice trailed off and he looked at Veronica.

Veronika's brow furrowed as she thought about the right way to express the situation. "Even the activities that were supposed to be for children were more for the adults," she said. "The parents do all the planning and make all the decisions. The kids just passively receive it all."

Vytautas sat quietly looking serious, and Birutė slowly shook her head.

"It's not like when we were in South America, and there were big rowdy family get-togethers, with lots of children running around playing games, and they were welcome right in the middle of the adults," said Jason. "It's more like Todd's wedding, we got banished to another room, and to be frank, his bride did not want us there at all. I have no idea why Todd thinks he's going to start a family with a woman who loathes children. For some reason he assumes that she'll want them when some sort of powerful urge is supposed to magically go off just before her biological clock runs out. If a miracle happens and she ever does get pregnant, those kids will be abused."

Veronika frowned. "Something's not right with her. She's jealous, and not in a normal way."

Jason rolled his eyes. "She has distorted perceptions of reality. Like the wedding party. She apparently had a good time for hours, then all it took was spotting our kids out the corner of her eye as we said 'goodbye' to a few folks, and she went hysterical. So now she's still telling every sympathetic ear she can reach that the whole evening was a nightmare."

Vytautas pushed his lower lip against the upper, and furrowed his eyebrow slightly. "So in other words, she had a good time, except for an incident late in the evening that might have lasted for what I take was a few minutes, and now she recounts the whole evening as an unqualified disaster."

Jason nodded.

"Unfortunately the part about distorting reality is actually fairly common," remarked Vytautas. "I would hazard a guess that it gets worse every time she complains about it."

Jason and Veronika both nodded.

Birutė looked troubled. "I fear that you're probably right about her. Jealousy and selfishness do not contribute to good parenting."

"Nor does her lack of emotional control," added Vytautas. "It's pretty common to see that the poster-children for 'brat camp', are usually the offspring of parents who are emotionally over-reactive. The reverse is also true. Good emotional self-control is what helps parents maintain benevolent control over situations.

"Good emotional control also contributes to success in life. Imagine the following scenario: a child has an accident with a glass of juice. The glass breaks, and the juice spills on some carpeting and upholstery.

"If the parent reacts with rage, the child is going to react with some mixture of fear or rage. Now imagine the grown-up child years later. Problems continue to trigger fear or rage. Rage leaves us ready for a fight. Fear, for no other options than running away from a problem. Strong negative emotions cut off access to our rational, creative, problem-solving skills and make us less resourceful.

Jason had never thought of it that way before. It seemed to be natural or at least understandable that parents get angry with their children when they misbehave, and Jason just assumed that not getting angry was a matter of self-control. But Vytautas was pointing out that emotions impel us into reptilian responses, and specifically, that anger motivates us for a fight. Once he put it that way, it seemed irrational for an able-bodied adult man to respond to a child as if to a threat.

"Parents who respond to a child's emotional outbursts by having one of their own are training their children to respond emotionally to other people's emotions," continued Vytautas. "How do you suppose that this trains the adult child to handle difficult people? In the future, some of those difficult people will happen to be bosses, customers, spouses, and someday, their own children."

Now this claim was easy for Jason to relate to. It seemed that most of the people who infused his life with unwanted drama were the ones whose negative emotions were out of control.

Vytautas paused before continuing. "There's a special case with boys. Parents tend to punish boys for expressing negative emotions more than they do girls.

"They also get teased and ridiculed by other kids at school for expressing even positive emotions.

"What happens is not what most people assume will happen. The boys don't learn to manage their emotions, they only learn to hide them."

Jason thought the same probably applied to himself. He was a typical male in that regard; he never felt comfortable expressing any emotions that might reveal vulnerabilities.

"What they're not learning to do is process their negative emotions, or for that matter, express their positive emotions to those who would appreciate them," continued Vytautas. "Often, when men get angry, it just builds up until the day it exceeds the limits of their ability to hide it, and they blow up."

Jason's thoughts immediately shifted to other men he knew. One was already prone to blowing up at odd moments. He started wondering if the other one were a ticking time bomb.

"But of course there was a problem even before he lost his temper," said Vytautas. "He has difficulty negotiating a solution or a compromise in a tense or confrontational situation, because he doesn't want to risk losing his temper if the conversation goes the wrong way. So, he just holds it in...until the day he doesn't."

Veronika looked alarmed at what Vytautas was telling her. "How should I prevent that with my sons?" she asked.

"Instead of becoming angry when a son is angry, you need to stay calm yourself, and either talk him through his anger, or, if it's too late for that, let it burn itself out and then talk to him about it later when he cools off," answered Birutė. "And it would help if fathers and older brothers would be respectful of his feelings. That doesn't mean they approve of any and all of his outbursts; it means they accept them and help talk him through to a resolution."

Veronika and Jason both nodded.

"Of course parents can't always be around their children, so they need to talk to them about what happens at school," continued Birutė. "That includes girls because girls can get bullied too."

"One of the most valuable gifts a parent can offer their children is to be someone they feel comfortable approaching about problems and bad feelings."

Birutė's words hit Jason hard. He'd never felt like he had anyone that he could confide in. He would have liked to have had a kindly mentor with whom he could talk about problems. None was to be had. He imagined approaching his own dad. It would have been an awkward conversation, and wouldn't have gotten very far before his dad would have excused himself to attend to more interesting matters. Todd? That would be like approaching a random stranger on the street. Doug? Jason had to stifle the urge to chortle. Yes, he could definitely approach Doug, in fact, Doug would certainly welcome the opportunity for Jason to confess his sins, followed by pronouncement of judgment and the imposition of a personal improvement plan.

Then a strange thought occurred to Jason. At first he wouldn't have even thought of going there. His mother? Out of the question, but why? Jason couldn't think clearly; the only thought that filled his head was what it felt like when she had turned cool towards him after the divorce.

Jason cleared his head and returned to the topic at hand. "OK, so getting back to dealing with problems…I understand that I should stay calm and respect children's feelings," he said. "What if I don't know what to say? Especially in the pressure of the moment!"

"I was wondering that too," confessed Veronika. "We're not hypnotists."

"If you don't know what to say, say as little as possible," advised Vytautas. "Get right to the point, and keep it short. Birutė knows a method of responding to common sorts of misbehavior that's easy to do."

"It's called 'three strikes and you're out'," explained Birutė. "If the child misbehaves, you say 'Strike one.' If the child continues misbehaving, you say 'Strike two.' On the third strike, you say 'Strike three. You're out,' and tell them what the consequences are and why they are being assigned, something like 'you continued running off and hiding after I told you to stay in my sight, so now you stand against this wall for a time-out.'"

Veronika looked scandalized. "Three strikes? You mean if my son swears at me or hits his sister, he gets to take another shot with impunity?"

Birutė laughed. "No. For serious offenses, you assign consequences immediately. But since many offenses are fairly minor until they escalate, it's a good way of nipping the problem in the bud."

Veronika thought about this. "Yeah, that might have been a good way of dealing with Angelina complaining about the food at the reception banquet. That started off as a small problem, but then it escalated."

"So by minor offenses, you mean whining...nagging...being mouthy or manipulative...?" asked Jason.

"You count all of those," answered Birutė. "It keeps them from escalating into something else."

"What do you think is appropriate for consequences?" asked Veronika. "Does it depend on how serious the offense is?"

"Interesting question," replied Vytautas. "The consequences should be enough to cancel out any reward from committing the offense, which is not necessarily proportional to the seriousness of the offense. You've probably already taken away the reward by interrupting the misbehavior, so it shouldn't take much to tip the scales in the balance of compliance. Most of the time, sitting in a corner or standing against a wall is enough."

"What about being sent to a bedroom?" asked Jason. "Don't a lot of parents do that?"

"Hmm...it might be better if they didn't," answered Birutė. "I've heard from parents who tried that, then their children resented being sent to bed at night! They felt like they were being punished. I always use a corner that the child won't have any other strong associations with. Let their bedroom be their sanctuary—a place of comfort and security for them."

"What if the child doesn't understand why you're counting strikes against him?" asked Jason. "Should you explain?"

"That's another interesting question," answered Vytautas. "You get better compliance if you give reasons, but it can also be distracting. Use your best judgment, and keep it brief. Sometimes it's also a good idea to explain the reason for a decision, because you're more likely to obtain consent if you give reasons."

Veronika frowned. "Doesn't that imply that the issue is open for negotiation?" she asked.

"They won't come to that conclusion if you issue a strike for badgering," said Birutė.

The cuckoo clock announced 9 o'clock. Jason and Vytautas had to get up early, so this was late for them. It had been a long conversation, though Jason thought it was worth it. Jason got up to clear the table, and Veronika excused herself to check on the children. Birutė and Vytautas insisted on helping Jason, so the kitchenette was tidied up by the time Veronika got back.

Good-byes were exchanged at the door.

Jason and Veronika found Kai awake. His excitement when they got to bed woke up Kaarina. She fussed briefly, but calmed down quickly after Veronika picked her up. Jason reached for her after crawling into bed, and put her down on his chest as he settled in to tell a bedtime story.

Jason's mind was still spinning after he finished the story. He had no idea how he was supposed to remember all of the suggestions that Vytautas and Birutė had given him. Then he remembered their advice about the three strikes method. That would be easy to remember. Too easy, in fact. Jason had doubts that such a simple scheme could work.

He also wondered about Veronika. Had she bought into it? He couldn't tell from her reactions; she might have just been going along just to be polite to the guests. Then he had a troubling thought: if she did have any concerns, maybe they were about Jason as a family leader. He couldn't blame her, because he didn't have a lot of confidence in himself either. He felt too little control over his own life to believe that he could make good decisions for anyone else.

He thought about this, and then decided that it was better to try and risk failure than to give up. For lack of better ideas, he would take the first step by taking Vytautas and Birutė's advice, and decide what to do next after seeing how that turned out.

Review

Words alone are quite powerful, but their power can be helpful or harmful depending on how the words are used.

Don't call names. Labeling tends to build up self-identities, and self-identities cause a lot of trouble, particularly in the teenage years. Even positive labels tend to backfire, because labels are static, but situations keep changing. Think about how many "good kids" get into trouble as teenagers or young adults.

Build and maintain positive rapport with your children, even when disciplining them.

Move reprimands promptly from the problem to the solution. Don't get stuck thinking and ranting about the problem. Solicit and wait for a firm commitment to the solution.

If you don't know what to say, say as little as possible. Most things parents say when angry and disappointed are more harmful than helpful. Even if you're reasonably calm, talking too much can be a distraction.

Use the "3 strikes and you're out" method to give feedback for minor misbehavior to help yourself and your

> child stay focused. It works best between the ages of when children first understand spoken commands through about 12 years old. By the time they are adolescents, they should have grown out of constant impulsive behaviors, or else you have a bigger problem outside the scope of this book. Reprimands and loss of privileges remain on the table, however, until they're adults.
>
> For serious offenses, interrupt the behavior and assign nonviolent consequences immediately.

Needed but not loved

Jason drove up to his brother's house to pick up Kai, Angelina, and Birutė. It was a fine old house, not quite a mansion but dating from a time when the city's engineers lived well and still had big families. The neighborhood had gone through tough times when heirs who had moved away rented rooms out to drug addicts and welfare dependents, but its proximity to desirable amenities eventually lured professionals back. Doug did a lot of work on it after he and Barbara bought it, restoring it to prime shape while maintaining its style and character.

Jason parked in the driveway, got out, and knocked on the door. Birutė answered. She looked troubled.

"Your brother came home early," she said. "Something is wrong. You might want to go talk to him while I get the children ready."

Jason raced up the stairs, tapped on the door of his brother's bedroom a few times, then went inside without waiting for an answer.

It was too dark to see anything. Jason was tempted to turn on the light, but then wondered if Doug might be sick and would not take kindly to having the light suddenly come on. He waited for his eyes to adjust, and then could just make out Doug's figure on the bed, lying on top of the covers, face down. He cautiously opened the door a little more to let in a little more light. Jason was worried for a moment, but then noticed his brother's chest convulsing. He approached, sat down on the side of the bed, and put a hand on his brother's shoulder. Now he could feel his brother's convulsions as he lay quietly sobbing.

Jason said nothing. For one thing, he thought that he already knew what the problem was. He assumed that Doug was once again overcome with grief over Barbara's sudden demise.

Jason had the feeling that Doug was fighting hard to suppress the sobbing. Jason was about to try and reassure Doug that it was OK to feel whatever he was feeling, but before he could lean over to whisper over Doug's ear, Doug forcefully turned around and faced Jason.

It took a few false starts for him to fight the sobbing long enough to spit out the words he was trying to express to Jason. Finally, he forced them: "Our...partner's...server crashed. They...didn't have...any backup. It's going to take...several weeks to get them back up...to where I can wire my code into theirs and hand it off to testing."

Jason was at a complete loss for how he was supposed to respond to what he just heard. Jason stroked Doug's shoulder reassuringly for several minutes while he pieced together what was going on.

Doug was already at his limit over the loss of Barbara. The setback at work pushed him over the edge. He was having a nervous breakdown.

Jason had to think some more to figure out how reasonable Doug's reaction was. Jason assumed that if the partner's server crashed, and they didn't have a backup, that probably wasn't any of Doug's doing.

Still, Jason wasn't sure that Doug wouldn't be blamed anyway, or at least be under all the more pressure to fix the problem as if it were his fault. Jason knew something about workplace bullying, and he also knew his brother to be quite rational. He had a feeling that Doug's job was almost certainly on the line.

Something still seemed wrong about the situation, regardless of how much pressure might have been put on Doug, or how much the fiasco might cost the company, or what his boss might do to him.

After several minutes of silent contemplation, Jason took a deep breath for courage, then finally spoke: "I understand that you've been feeling a lot of stress. It's been a tough time for you. I would like to help you get through this…"

"You can't," interrupted Doug, shaking his head. "There's nothing you can do. That module is already a month late. I'm not welcome to help them reconstruct the missing codebase because there's proprietary stuff involved. I am absolutely dead in the water for the next two, more likely three weeks, and that will put us at least another month behind schedule."

"That's not the kind of help I had in mind to offer," Jason said. "I'm talking about moral support…"

Doug shook his head again. "Moral support is not going to get the project delivered any faster or in any better shape. I don't think you're listening to me…"

Jason listened quietly, nodding from time to time, for three minutes as Doug explained the details of the missing module, what it was supposed to do, and even started getting into the potential market impact of the delay.

Doug ended with "...and you can't even help yourself, so I don't see how you can possibly help me."

Jason realized that Doug was not receptive to anything he could say about the matter. He decided to postpone stating the obvious until at least such time as Doug was in a calmer mood.

"OK, I guess there's nothing I can do to help," said Jason as agreeably as possible. "Let's just head back to my place for some supper."

Doug looked at Jason for a few moments, then stared off into space. "No, I'm not in the mood."

"OK, you don't have to eat with us, but I don't think it would be wise to leave you alone with your thoughts," said Jason.

"That's fine," said Doug. "You can find something to eat in the kitchen."

"Stay here?" asked Jason, realizing full well what was expected, but playing innocent. "At the very least I need to take Birutė home. And to be honest, supper is waiting for the rest of us."

"Doesn't she live just a few blocks from you? Have her drive herself home in your car," Doug suggested helpfully.

"Birutė doesn't drive," said Jason, "I mean, she doesn't know how."

Doug looked confused for a moment. Then he finally gave in. "OK, I guess I don't want to keep Birutė waiting...Give me a few minutes to get ready."

The whole scenario was stranger than usual, but Jason was relieved that the matter was resolved. Thankfully, Doug was relenting for the sake of Birutė, not himself.

Birutė looked up anxiously when she saw Jason and Doug enter the room, then sensing the problem was resolved, she quickly recovered and looked relieved. She and the kids were playing a game, but had jackets and shoes on. She reminded the kids that she had warned them the game might end abruptly, and they helped her put the game away without a fuss. They were hungry and ready to leave on their own account.

Birutė considerately took the back center seat in the car to reduce the likelihood of bickering between Angelina and Kai. Her attention was the prize they contended over. Angelina demanded and got the lion's share but didn't put up a fuss when Birutė reminded her that Kai was allowed a share of attention as well.

Doug sat in the front passenger seat sulking. Jason didn't mind since his brother's low energy level meant that he didn't have enough to spare criticizing Jason's driving. It was almost a quiet, uneventful drive to Jason's place, except that a fight broke out only a few blocks from Birutė's apartment.

It escalated faster than Birutė could intervene, and neither child was listening to her. That meant they both had to be given feedback. Jason's reaction was immediate: he veered off the arterial onto a quieter residential street, pulled the car over, and stopped.

Doug suddenly found enough energy to react. "What the hell are you doing?"

Jason's feeling of being in control suddenly evaporated. He wondered if he had erred by stopping to deal with the situation instead of just putting up with it the last few blocks in order to accommodate Doug's expectations. He wondered if it mattered—

then it started occurring to him that Angelina's behavior always deteriorated after spending any significant time with her father. That posed a lose-lose dilemma.

Luckily Birutė intervened. She put a hand on Doug's shoulder to get his attention and said: "It's OK, Doug; Jason knows what he's doing. He's doing exactly what he's supposed to."

Jason felt his self-confidence return. He got out of the car, opened the door on Kai's side, and escorted Kai to one of the trees lining the street. Birutė took charge of Angelina.

"I didn't start it!" huffed Kai.

"I didn't either," said Jason mildly. "But my ride was interrupted too." Jason considered that Kai probably felt resentful that he was being punished for something that Angelina started. He got down on his knees to get closer to Kai's level, and looked him in the eye. "You weren't listening to Birutė when she tried to talk to you, were you?"

Kai looked down. Jason patted him on the shoulder reassuringly.

After the brief time-out, the kids were escorted back to the car. Doug still looked grumpy, but he was calm and quiet. There were no more interruptions the few remaining blocks to Birutė's apartment.

Both kids demanded hugs from Birutė before she got out of the car. Doug expressed surprise, because it did not seem in character for Angelina to attach herself to anyone. He looked even more surprised when Angelina expressed reluctance to part company, despite having received a time-out just a few minutes earlier. She was known for holding grudges. Jason figured that since Birutė had never expressed any negative emotions when doling out the time-out, Angelina didn't get as worked up as usual, so there was no lingering resentment.

"Well, what are you waiting for?" Doug asked Jason irritably.

"Huh? Oh, I always wait until she's safely inside," answered Jason. He continued watching Birutė. Something seemed to be wrong. She was fumbling with her purse a long time.

Doug informed Jason that she was a big girl and he was acting foolishly, but Jason's attention remained on Birutė. He rolled down the window and yelled to her. She approached looking chagrined.

"I can't find my keys!" she said. Jason detected anxiety in her voice.

He opened his door and was about to get out when he felt Doug's hand grab his shoulder and tug. Not hard enough to pull him back in, but Jason understood the implied order, relaxed, and turned his head to face Doug, who ignored him as he rolled down his window and motioned for Birutė.

She peeked into Doug's window. "I'm sure I don't have my keys! I don't know where they could be...I haven't used them since I left home this morning," she said, flustered.

"Don't worry. You'll find them," Doug said reassuringly. "Just get back in the car, and we'll go to Jason's house. You can just wait there until your husband gets home to let you in." He was smiling and looked uncharacteristically friendly towards one of his hapless younger brother's hapless friends.

It was apparent that his mood was improving. He enjoyed playing the hero.

Birutė looked mildly upset, but obeyed. It was a fairly respectable neighborhood, but she was tired, and it was getting late in the day.

Jason, for his part, was relieved that the problem was resolved. He drove a few more blocks to the fisherman's cottage, parked the car, and collected the children. He was surprised to notice his brother behaving chivalrously towards Birutė, helping her out of the car and closing the car door behind her. He was still smiling.

Birutė still seemed a little flustered as she accompanied the rest of the group into the house, but the excited squeals of the children as they raced in, and Veronika's cheerful reaction to the surprise guests distracted her.

Everyone was talking at once as the group made its way from the entry hall towards the kitchen end of the day-room. Birutė started apologizing for the imposition, while Jason reassured her that it was no trouble. Veronika told her to leave a message for Vytautas to come and join the rest of them for dinner, and Doug tried unsuccessfully to shove a cell phone into her hand.

Birutė objected that there were too many people to expect Veronika to serve all of them. There was, in fact, no dinner in sight. Veronika insisted that it would be fun to work on it together. Doug intervened and informed them that he would take care of dinner. Both women turned to each other surprised, but then broke out in grins and giggles, and took him up on his offer.

Doug took his cell phone and called out for gourmet pizza. Then he asked Birutė what her home phone number was. He dialed it in as she told him. Then she looked surprised that he did not hand the phone over to her, but started talking.

Apparently, Vytautas was already home. Without bothering to explain the situation, Doug ordered him to stay put and he and Jason would be over to pick him up in a few minutes.

Birutė's mood improved as the pressure to come up with dinner for nine people was resolved. The fisherman's cottage was getting a bit crowded, but after noticing Herbert sitting in the corner of the room looking increasingly excited about having company, she and Veronika gathered the children and went to sit with him while they all waited for the boys to bring back the pizza.

Meanwhile, Jason was worried about how his brother might treat Vytautas. He reasonably anticipated that his brother might take a condescending view of his "little brother's little friends." Vytautas and Birutė were certainly not the kinds of people that Doug and Barbara associated with. Despite years spent in London, they still came off as immigrant bumpkins. Vytautas's sophistication in matters of pop-psychology was not matched in topics more pertinent to cocktail parties. Birutė was spared critical scrutiny probably due solely to chivalry. As a young buck, Vytautas would not necessarily be spared Doug's potentially ornery and patronizing behavior.

Jason drove himself and Doug back to Vytautas's apartment, and he came scurrying out the door to their car.

"'Evening, gents. What's going on?" he asked.

"We're going to pick up some pizzas I ordered. You're coming with us," said Doug matter-of-factly.

Jason filled in all the details regarding Birutė not being able to find her keys, coming to his house, and Doug hosting pizza for everyone as Vytautas got into the car.

"Much obliged," said Vytautas. "Birutė needn't worry about her keys. I found them."

Vytautas might have been left wondering what Doug was doing in the neighborhood. Jason had never explicitly explained that the protocol was always for Jason to show up at Doug's house when summoned, but Vytautas knew enough about their relationship to have sensed that something out-of-the-ordinary was happening.

Introductions were brief. "Doug, Vytautas." Jason didn't want to try his brother's patience with formalities instead of listening to his instructions for getting to the pizza restaurant. Doug surprised Jason by reaching around as well as he could in the tight confines of the car, and extending a hand to Vytautas. Jason peaked up at the rear-view mirror just in time to catch a glimpse of Vytautas's face expressing pain and embarrassment for not being able to handle Doug's crushing grip. Despite his geeky personality, Doug had a naturally stocky, muscular build—and perhaps a need to show Vytautas who was boss in case it wasn't already obvious.

Jason followed his brother's driving instructions and ended up near a trendy neighborhood center where the pizza restaurant was located. There were no parking lots, so they had to find the nearest street parking and walk a few blocks. The restaurant had no street-level storefront; you had to know to go up a flight of stairs from street-level. Jason was used to such venues even if he couldn't afford them, but Vytautas was showing signs of feeling out-of-place. There was a sweeping view of the nearby lake and surrounding neighborhood out the window. The pizzas were gourmet quality, the owner having grown up working at his parents' restaurant on Capri.

Doug too must have thought the situation unusual, because he volunteered an explanation while they sat waiting for their pizzas. He gave Vytautas a frank account of the incident at work that touched off the series of events leading to the impromptu get-together.

Vytautas listened politely while Doug told the story all the way through to the catastrophizing.

"Are you worried you might lose your job over this?" asked Vytautas.

"Well, of course I am!" answered Doug. He went on to explain how the software industry expected results, not excuses.

"I understand why you're worried. There's a lot at stake," said Vytautas. "Do you have a plan for getting another job if you lose this one?"

Doug sighed. "I haven't thought about that yet. Right now, I'm still thinking about how I can cut my losses on the project as it is."

Vytautas nodded. "You're very dedicated to your job. I hope your bosses appreciate that."

Doug looked puzzled for a moment. "No," he said, "that's not one of their concerns. If I weren't dedicated, they'd just fire me. They're very bottom-line oriented."

Vytautas nodded. "As they should be. No profits, no job. But profits come from delivering products that delight customers. I would imagine that you're not really as replaceable as they would like to think. If they let you go, they'll be throwing away a great deal of familiarity and expertise with the system."

Doug gave Vytautas a sober look and nodded.

"So the problem isn't really that you're expendable," concluded Vytautas." The problem is that non-technical managers have little sense of the full extent of your value to the company, so they fail to treat you accordingly."

Doug looked puzzled again. "Even if what you're saying is true—and maybe it is" he conceded, "I'm not sure it's relevant. I'll still be out of a job."

Vytautas nodded. "And it's good that you're thinking about the worst-case scenario, because that helps put the problem into perspective. Now that you've accepted the worst of it, you can take your attention off the problem and re-direct it to finding solutions."

Doug continued looking perplexed as he worked the situation over in his mind. "Is the problem the horrible shape my project is in, or is the problem finding another job?" he wondered aloud.

"Well, they're both problems, but the first problem isn't your problem," answered Vytautas. "And since there's not much you can do about your boss's problem, it would make sense to think about your own problem first. If you did have to find another job, you could do that, couldn't you?"

Doug considered it for just a moment, then said: "It would be difficult to cover up the fact that I was fired."

Vytautas nodded. "Difficult, but not impossible. From what Jason tells me about you, I imagine that your depth of technical skills and experience makes you very competitive. You don't really see yourself as unemployable and out on the street, do you? It sounds like your unease is mostly a matter of facing the unknown."

Doug thought about it, and concluded that indeed he was unlikely to end up unemployable. He would be able to get another job. Probably not an optimal situation; he'd have to take whatever he could find. He exhaled forcefully, then expressed that perhaps it was time for a change.

He said nothing more as he turned briefly to Vytautas, then his attention was diverted to the waiter who arrived with the boxes of pizza and salads.

"Let's take these to the car, and then we'll pop into the supermarket to get some drinks," said Doug.

"I ordered the closest thing to plain cheese for the kids and, ah, Herbert," Doug said, chuckling as he considered that blue-collar Herbert might not care for some of the more exotic types. "The rest are an assortment of some of their signature toppings. All the ones I chose are meatless. Jason mentioned that you were experimenting with vegetarianism," he said to Vytautas. Like many geeky computer programmers, Doug had an excellent memory for casually-mentioned details.

Vytautas blushed. "That's very kind of you to consider me. Yes, I've been toying with the idea under the influence of the leader of my order. I don't mean for you to go to any trouble on my account. In fact, I didn't expect to be treated at all."

"Your order…" echoed Doug distractedly trying to make sense of what Vytautas had just said. It wasn't too hard for Jason to guess what his brother was thinking. Order, as in Royal Order of the Knights of the Round Table? And they're vegetarians? Vegetarian knights? Really? Or at least the ringleader is. Then Doug turned to Vytautas and smiled. "No trouble."

"Yes, my order," repeated Vytautas enthusiastically. "Our leader is the one who suggested the martial arts training I'm trying to talk Jason into."

"That's very interesting," said Doug. "You know, maybe if I do get fired...or quit...I'll have more time to take care of myself. Maybe a little martial arts training would get me conditioned."

"What style of martial arts is it?" he asked. "Is it Aikido? I know that's popular around here."

Vytautas suddenly looked a bit flustered. "Well...ah, no...the leader of my order said Aikido tends to be more of a ritualistic performance art than actual fighting. He says those demonstrations where one man takes on several attackers are choreographed and unrealistic. He suggested Jiu-Jitsu as a more serious option for self-defense."

Doug raised his eyebrows in surprise. "To be honest, I wouldn't have known that. I take it the leader of your order is pretty serious then." Doug knit his eyebrows in thought, and then he said, "I'm up for a challenge. I'll sign up as soon as the uncertainty over my employment is resolved."

The pizzas were delivered to the car, and while they were at it, Jason fetched some bags from his trunk to carry drinks in.

Doug escorted Vytautas and Jason to the booze section of a small, urban, upscale supermarket in the basement under some luxury view condominiums. It was a small section, but quality was good to excellent—and the price expensive. Standing between them, he put an arm around each of their shoulders, tugged them a little closer, and asked: "What will it be, boys? Get whatever you like!"

Vytautas blushed deeply.

Doug looked at him. "It's OK, Bud. My treat."

"Cheers, mate," Vytautas said. "You are very generous. Unfortunately, I know absolutely nothing about wine. I think you had better choose something."

Doug looked surprised. "English, and don't drink?" he said incredulously. Vytautas turned to him with a shy grin on his face.

Jason intervened. "You're right that he picked up the accent in London, but he's not English. I drank a little wine in Mendoza, and sometimes I have a beer, but I don't think any of us drink all that much. Maybe some sparkling water would be a better choice, especially around the kids."

"Water would be fine for us," said Vytautas sheepishly.

Doug laughed good-naturedly and escorted Vytautas and Jason to a non-alcoholic beverage section, where they picked up some flavored sparkling mineral water before paying for the goods and heading back to the car. It was a quick drive home again.

By the time they got back to the fisherman's cottage, everyone was hungry, so Angelina and Kai fairly pounced on their fathers when they arrived. Boxes were quickly set down and popped open on the dining table and spare tray tables that Herbert happened to have from his years of eating in front of the television, alone or with a few old pals from the shipyards.

"Oh!" Birutė squealed as she saw the contents of the boxes. There was a vegetable salad consisting of shaved fennel bulbs, radicchio, and toasted walnuts. The pizzas included a Margherita made from fresh tomatoes, basil, and real buffalo mozzarella; a Sicilian-style scacciata stuffed with savory greens; and pizza vegetariana topped with mysterious ingredients like eggplant, artichoke hearts, and hot peppers.

Birutė and Vytautas expressed that they had never had such exotic fare in their lives.

Plates and utensils were quickly passed around. Formalities were dispensed with, and the atmosphere was festive.

Jason couldn't help noticing Doug's mood. Doug's default way of engaging the world was with a slightly cool manner, the minimum effort to seem acceptably polite but with a touch of directness, punctuated at times with a certain restrained impatience that was noticeable when dealing with intellectual inferiors, or with social inferiors like Jason. He never blew up, and most of the time his emotions were restrained if indeed detectable at all, but he sometimes bordered on expressions of disappointment or frustration.

Nevertheless, he was the only family member who was ever affectionate towards Jason, sometimes giving him a side-hug when he was in a good mood.

He was in one of those uncommon moods right now. He had Angelina sitting on his lap trying to monopolize his attention while he carried on a warm and friendly conversation with Herbert of all people.

To Jason, this seemed unexpected. He was still grieving for Barbara, and he'd had a nervous breakdown earlier in the day. He'd only recently met Herbert and Vytautas, so it wasn't like he was among dear old friends.

Jason considered the course of events, and suspected it was getting to play big-daddy. Doug wasn't particularly warm and friendly, but he was quite generous. That was one characteristic Jason liked about his brother.

Of course, Doug was generous by default, but it didn't usually propel him into such a good mood. Something was different this time. Jason considered this a few seconds, then realized that Doug was warming up to company that was a lot less jaded and more appreciative than his usual social and professional circles.

Jason didn't think that Doug was stuck-up. If he did more of what he wanted to instead of what he thought he had to, it seemed to Jason that Doug would have spent more time with family and real friends. For that matter, he suspected that Barbara hadn't been stuck-up either; otherwise, she wouldn't have associated with some of the riff-raff in her parenting circles, nor would she have taken the initiative to engage Jason and Veronika at the wedding party. They hobnobbed with their snooty friends only because they thought they had to for the sake of their careers. It worked for Barbara, but truth be told she was more socially adept than Doug. Doug's social skills weren't commensurate with his ability to design and code complex software systems.

Jason's ruminations suddenly dissipated as he sensed himself being mentioned in conversation. He listened carefully to determine the context.

It was Doug who had mentioned his name. Jason had been recruited on one of his projects.

"What are we doing?" asked Jason.

"Not right now, silly, tomorrow," answered Doug. "You have the day off, and miraculously, so do I."

At least now Jason knew when. What and where might be difficult to tease out without interrupting Doug and sidetracking the conversation. Jason considered that spending a little time with his brother might not be a bad thing, so as long as they weren't doing something dangerous or unethical like robbing a bank. Jason thought he could keep still and pay attention for more clues.

"But I don't understand why you need so many gifts," said Birutė. "How many children's birthdays are you celebrating all at once?"

Doug chuckled. "Just one. But there will be at least ten kids there."

Now Vytautas and Birutė were both looking at him with even more puzzled looks on their faces.

Jason suspected that there was some sort of gross misunderstanding at play, whereby each of the two sides of the conversation was stuck inside his own sense of reality, without understanding the other side. He decided to risk looking like an idiot if his hunch was wrong: "Doug, I don't think they understand why you need to buy every child at the party a gift instead of just one gift for the guest of honor."

Doug rolled his eyes. "Well, you can't just treat one kid and not the others. That's not fair. You wouldn't want the other kids to feel left out."

Doug then gave Jason a hard, serious look. "You know, you really need to learn to think about and respect other people's feelings."

Jason nodded. Now he understood what he would be doing tomorrow, and Birutė and Vytautas had a shot at understanding the reasoning behind why they were going shopping tomorrow to buy ten or so gifts for one child's birthday party.

"And we're going to take the kids," Doug continued resolutely. "All of them, including Kaarina. Veronika could use a break now and then." Veronika beamed. She was quite a trooper but even so she did appreciate the prospect of a day to get things done at a relaxed pace and having a little time left over for herself.

"That's mighty thoughtful of you, bro," said Jason.

Jason was a little worried about discipline falling apart while his brother was in charge.

While Barbara was alive, Doug had always let her handle discipline, except to intervene when she lost her temper with the girls. If Birutė or even Veronika were accompanying them, he would have deferred to either of them, but Jason had a feeling that Doug would over-rule him instantly if he tried to keep Angelina in line.

And the locale was a particular challenge: Angelina's favorite shopping mall. It was an old suburban-style shopping mall that survived and continued evolving after the aging and urbanization of the surrounding neighborhood. The original mall had been build along an outdoor corridor, but was later covered over with a roof and skylights to imitate the indoor shopping corridor of other shopping malls. The Kentia palms planted in the 1950s were now tall trees, and growing around their bases were Ti plants, Heliconias, Hibiscus, and other colorful plants. Sculptural fountains of the same era were still operating, but the individual stores and cafés had come and gone. The current mix was typical of higher-end shopping malls nationwide, with a lot of the trendiest fashions, toys, and food.

As the mall expanded, it started including uncovered alleys lined with small, independent shops quaintly decorated with window boxes and hanging baskets overflowing with Impatiens, Begonias, and Lobelias. The alleys intersected covered but not entirely enclosed corridors also lined with shops, creating an upstairs-downstairs, indoor-outdoor excursion.

Today the morning had started a bit cool for the season, and there was a forecast of a slight chance of light rain that Doug had warned them to prepare for just for good measure. There was only a thin cloud-cover, that would probably burn off by noon to leave a mildly warm, sunny afternoon typical of the season. If there were no problems with the kids, there were excellent prospects for a pleasant outing.

"And just like the bridges of Königsberg, it's impossible to pass by every store without revisiting any section," said Doug as they walked through the mall. "If you think of the corridors and alleys as being the edges of a graph, and the intersections of the corridors and alleys being nodes, then to visit any node, you need an even number of edges, one for coming, and one for going.

"The possible exceptions are the starting node and the ending node. But you only have one start, and one end. So if you have more than two nodes with an odd number of edges intersecting it, then logically you can't traverse the whole graph without traversing at least one of the edges more than once."

"That's very interesting," said Jason distractedly. Truth be told, the only part that registered was the suggestion that they would be passing by every shop in the complex, and some of them more than once. His attention was elsewhere.

"You're not going to pick that are you?" he asked suddenly, raising the volume of his voice just slightly, and dropping the pitch.

Angelina looked startled. "I'm just looking!" she said defensively, holding a Hibiscus blossom that she had been just about to dislodge.

"OK. You look with your eyes, not with your hands," commented Jason matter-of-factly.

"Huh? What's wrong?" asked Doug.

Jason smiled and turned to him. "Nothing's wrong. Just a little reminder to respect the mall owners' property."

To his credit, Doug had a strong sense of property rights, plus Jason hadn't sounded angry, so Doug apparently decided to hold his tongue regarding being excessively strict with the kids. He started to think out loud regarding a plan of action for shopping.

"I don't know what we're looking for," he said. "I know the guest of honor. She's a little older than Angelina, but they have a great time together, and they like a lot of the same things. So I've decided to let Angelina be the arbiter of taste and interest."

There was some wisdom in this plan. Angelina tended to know what she wanted, and was fairy capable of taking the initiative to find it.

Angelina zoomed in on the first prospect fairly quickly. As soon as it was in sight, she ran to a small toy store that specialized in the latest and most popular toys. Doug didn't seem to be alarmed that she had run so far ahead of the rest of them, but Jason was worried about the lack of supervision, not to mention her safety. He picked up his pace as quick as he could with his daughter in a stroller. He looked back a few times to make sure that Kai was with Doug.

His heart raced a little when he did not spot her immediately in the store, but he calmed down after finding her standing behind a stack of toys. She was handling the display model.

The toy was a plush, long-necked unicorn. Around its neck was a necklace covered in diamond-like zircons. Its mane was full of long tresses styled like a human female's, its un-natural candy colors tied in ribbons.

"I want one too!" squealed Angelina. "Oh...please...I'll be good!"

Jason picked up one of the boxes and read the description. It had an electronic chip in it; essentially a mini-computer. It was voice-activated and could respond to certain commands, questions, and statements with its voice synthesizer. If you talked nicely to it, it responded with affirmations and praise. It could also be integrated with a game running on a computer or pad, that featured the same licensed character and others like it.

It cost $495. Accessories extra.

Jason turned to Doug, who had caught up with them. "By any chance did you specify what kind of price you had in mind before we started?"

"Huh? Not really," answered Doug. "Not too keen on buying a toy that spies on her, either."

Now the situation was awkward. Telling Angelina "no" was never easy. Jason wondered whether Doug would buy the electronic abomination just to avoid a tantrum.

"Well now what do we do?" asked Doug. He caught Jason by surprise by abdicating responsibility—to Jason. In retrospect, he should have seen it coming. Doug had a habit of never making any uncomfortable parenting decisions.

Jason realized he would have to fight battles on two different fronts, but he took over anyway. Someone had to, or the situation would never resolve satisfactorily.

"Angelina, didn't we come here to buy a gift for Laura?" he asked. He was tempted to point out that it was her birthday, not Angelina's, but he decided the less said, the better. He waited for an answer.

Angelina didn't answer him. She continued badgering her father. "I want it! I want it!" Despite her intelligence, Angelina was acting like a three-year-old.

Jason realized that he was not in rapport with Angelina, so he got down on her level and tried to make eye contact. For her part, Angelina evaded it, and instead tried to engage her father, tugging on his shirt. "I want it, I want it!" she continued.

"Strike one," said Jason.

This time Angelina reacted to what he said, but not in an entirely positive way. She shoved the box back into the display, huffy.

Doug was about to say something, probably trying to reason with her or appease her. Jason held up a hand and gave him a "wise" look. Doug hesitated, then lost his nerve. Later, Jason would explain to him that when emotions are on the edge, it's best to say as little as possible, and wait it out.

Angelina actually recovered, as Jason sensed she would. She looked angry, but held her tongue. She headed for the door of the store, intending to storm out. Jason thought that was actually not a bad idea, since apparently he and his brother needed to have a little chat.

He headed to a bench, and parked the stroller next to himself. Kai tagged along behind. Jason motioned for Angelina to stay close. She did, scowling.

Jason looked up at Doug, who looked back with a mixture of embarrassment and defensiveness.

"Here's something that Vytautas and Birutė taught me," said Jason. "If you get buy-in from kids before-hand, then later they'll be more likely to accept decisions that would otherwise be unpopular. How about if you tell Angelina right now how much money you're willing to spend for a gift to the birthday girl?"

Jason waited for an answer. Doug just glared back. As the seconds ticked away, it started occurring to Jason that he had just stumbled into a sore point that was probably significant.

Then it hit him: Doug can't enforce limits on Angelina.

Well, of course, he could. The question was why he was unwilling to do so.

Jason instinctively realized that now was not the time to find out, because Doug's and Angelina's patience was wearing thin. Instead, it was time to de-escalate the situation and resolve the immediate impasse regarding the selection of an appropriate gift.

Jason decided to take the initiative. He slapped Doug playfully on the shoulder and said: "Come on. I have an idea."

The rest of his group followed him, two of them grumpy but complying. A few minutes later they ended up in front of a game shop.

It was extremely popular with geeks. Doug's own mood improved suddenly, though his face betrayed signs of sheepishness. They were supposed to be buying a gift for a little girl, not him.

Jason pointed out that there was a corner devoted to games suitable for children and for families. Everyone started looking for the right game, Angelina the least enthusiastically. Jason found something, but Doug over-ruled him with his own choice. At least now Jason had Doug's buy-in.

The game was paid for, but Doug looked concerned as they exited the shop. "Well, we got a present for the guest-of-honor, but now what shall we get for the rest of the kids?" he asked.

"Hmmm...how about a piece of birthday cake...or a cupcake?" asked Jason.

"No, silly, something to open," said Doug.

"Doug, yesterday you told me that I needed to be more sensitive to other people's feelings. I'd like to learn that. Explain to me what the feelings are that I need to be more sensitive to. I'm kind of an insensitive lout," Jason said straight-faced.

"Well, how would you feel if you watched some other kid opening a present, but you didn't get one? You'd feel left out, wouldn't you?" answered Doug just as seriously as Jason had asked.

"No, I wouldn't feel left out, in fact, I didn't feel anything was wrong when I didn't get to open any presents because it wasn't my birthday. I seem to recall taking it for granted that's the way it worked," answered Jason.

"Well, people are more empathetic nowadays," said Doug. "I guess you just didn't learn," he added after sighing.

Jason decided that he wasn't going to make any headway on the issue, so he decided the next best thing would be to compromise. "How about if Veronika and I made something?" he asked.

Doug raised a skeptical eyebrow. "That sounds cheap."

"That's right, it doesn't have to be expensive; it can just be nice," said Jason.

Doug sighed again and gave in. Truth be told he didn't particularly enjoy shopping, especially because it held a lot of associations with humiliation every time Angelina threw a temper tantrum in public. This time the tantrum was avoided, but it would be a while before that association wore off.

Jason calculated that it was about time that Kaarina would need to use the toilet. She wasn't quite toilet-trained yet, but if he paid attention to her cycles, he could often get her to use the toilet. Next destination was the restrooms. On the way they encountered about a dozen young people, mostly teens, coming from the opposite direction. Something seemed out of place to Jason; they weren't talking or interacting with each other, but Jason had the feeling that they were, in fact, a group. The realization came too late; the group attacked them once they were surrounded.

One girl went for Angelina's package, and another for her back-pack. She screamed and instinctively drew herself tight. A young man grabbed Kai, and two others came at Jason. He sensed that regardless of whatever else they intended, they were going to assault him. Jason felt extremely vulnerable, because he was not only outnumbered, but pushing a toddler in a stroller.

He had no idea what to do.

Luckily, Doug's protective instincts kicked in. He grabbed Angelina tight and swung her forcefully out of the hands of the girls trying to grab her stuff. One of them who didn't get out of the way in time lost her balance and landed on the ground. She screamed, but her scream was followed by laughter as she was seized up in the excitement of the situation.

Still holding Angelina, Doug then charged the man who was holding Kai. The man dropped Kai and prepared to confront Doug. Doug let go of Angelina seconds before plowing right into the man who had grabbed Kai, sending him crashing to the ground. Doug did not appear the least bit fazed.

The commotion had sufficiently distracted the men confronting Jason that he'd been able to back away. He pushed Kaarina's stroller away and stood between it and the action. Unfortunately, one of the two men was now eying Jason again, while the other turned his attention to Doug. Doug charged again, going for the man who was still confronting Jason. He turned to face Doug, while his partner reached for Doug's neck from behind.

Doug didn't react to having a man grab his throat. He deflected the blow from the man facing him, then knocked him down. Doug then flipped the man behind him over his own body, sending him tumbling onto the one in front of him.

It was over. The portion of the pack who had been circling the action looking for an opening, but never quite built up enough nerve to go in for the attack, were fleeing, while the remaining participants began withdrawing. But Doug kept watching, turning his gaze this way or that looking for anyone who still wanted to fight.

Jason checked on each of the kids. Kaarina was calm. Didn't seem to realize what had just happened. Angelina was more in a fighting mood than upset. This was one of those times when her spitfire personality came in handy. Kai expressed relief; he didn't know why he'd been grabbed but apparently realized that the man who did it was up to no good.

Doug's defensive posture faded slowly as the attackers retreated, and then it was like nothing happened.

Jason assessed the situation. There was no evidence of any remaining threat, but he thought it prudent to remain at a heightened sense of alertness. Aside from that, something else was bothering him. What would have happened if Doug had not been present to defend them?

Once in the men's room, Jason patiently held Kaarina over the toilet. It took a few minutes, but success! Jason gave Kaarina a big smile. "Good job going potty!" he said. She squealed excitedly back. After the restroom break, Doug suggested lunch before leaving the mall. Jason was a little concerned with how long they'd be out with Kaarina, but he also realized that Angelina and Kai would be hungry, so he deferred to popular opinion which was overwhelmingly favorable to lunch. Doug treated them to a local chain restaurant that had typical fast-food menu items but of a much better grade than typical of fast-food restaurants. The hamburgers, pizza, and fish-and-chips could all be reasonably described as "gourmet quality." The restaurant had a pleasant outdoor patio, but Doug decided they'd stay indoors when he noticed the increasing humidity and gathering clouds.

By the time they were finished eating, a light rain was already falling, and it looked like a lot more was on the way. Angelina pulled off her small backpack and rummaged around for a light sweater and a tiny folding umbrella. Doug pulled a rain poncho out of his hip-pack. Jason quickly pulled out a stroller cover that he kept handy in the storage compartment under the stroller; it would keep Kaarina dry and snug. As he finished putting it over the stroller, he was startled by Doug muttering swear words.

Kai had no jacket or any rain gear at all. Not even after being explicitly told by his uncle to grab a jacket before they left.

Doug wasn't swearing particularly at Kai, but he was obviously irritated. Jason considered this and suspected that he was embarrassed to look like a negligent adult for having a child in his company who was not dressed properly for the weather. For his part, Jason scolded himself for not verifying that Kai had heeded his uncle's warning.

Kai looked upset and ashamed. Jason got down to his eye level, put his hands on Kai's shoulders, and reassured him that uncle wasn't really angry at him, and was just upset because he didn't want him to be cold and wet. Then he stood up again, and took off his own windbreaker that was thin but water-repellent, and had a hood folded into its zippered collar. He pulled out the hood, and then wrapped Kai up in it as snugly as he could, tucking it here and there to keep it from tripping Kai.

Because he hadn't expected the weather to turn as cool and rainy as it had, Jason himself had only a thin, short-sleeved shirt under the windbreaker. The rain became heavier before they got to the bus stop, and then they had to wait for the bus.

Doug gave him a hard stare. Jason had no idea what he was thinking until at length he said: "I'm better insulated than you are. Take my poncho."

Jason smiled good-naturedly. "It's OK. I don't mind getting wet so that Kai can stay warm and dry".

Doug continued staring at Jason. Jason suspected that he was considering whether to insist or not. Luckily the bus came before he had to consider much longer.

When they got home, Jason slipped into the bedroom, set Kaarina down on the bed, and then put on a dry shirt. Veronika never noticed because she was preoccupied in the day-room, where Birutė was teaching her how to sew.

After Jason and Kaarina joined everyone else, he explained about the party favors. Birutė's eyes lit up. She had an idea. She called Vytautas and had him bring over some craft items, including some construction paper and origami paper. Veronika took Kaarina back and just watched the construction of the party favors after a table was set up to work on.

Angelina complained to Birutė about how her choice of gifts had been over-ruled. Birutė listened sympathetically for a while, then snuck in a few leading questions designed to get Angela to think about other perspectives. Jason was impressed at how well she was managing Angelina with empathy and respect. Doug wasn't paying enough attention to notice. He sort of took for granted that Angelina behaved better for Birutė, because "that was her job."

Soon Angelina was helping to assemble the party favors and even seemed to enjoy the process.

Seeing that Veronika had no dinner plans, Doug called for Chinese takeout. The mood was festive, and everyone, including Angelina, had a good time.

After dinner, a card game. Birutė reminded Angelina that you win some and lose some. Angelina sighed and said that she'd try not to get upset if she lost.

"You're sure?" asked Birutė. She was after a firm commitment.

"YES, I'm sure!" Angelina huffed, then rolled her eyes. Birutė smiled, but Doug looked upset.

Jason noticed his brother's expression and asked what was wrong.

"I don't know if this is a good game for children. It's too competitive," Doug answered.

Birutė, Vytautas, and Veronica all looked puzzled. Jason suppressed a wise grin and asked: "Are you worried about how she'll feel if she loses?"

Doug gave Jason a scandalized look and asked "Don't you remember what I said about being more considerate of other people's feelings?"

Before Jason could answer, Vytautas stepped in to bail him out. "Being considerate of other people's feelings does not imply being able to control them. Nobody can control anyone else's feelings, only their own. Everyone needs to learn how to respond appropriately to setbacks."

Doug looked skeptical. Birutė, despite her demure personality, shared her own thoughts. "Learning how to deal with losses is a valuable lesson. You wouldn't want to deprive her of that, would you?".

Doug didn't answer. He had his own idea. He and Angelina would play "as a team." Doug was by far the best and most brutally competitive player.

The game seemed to be going quite well. Most of the players seemed to be enjoying it, despite squeals of embarrassment over their performance against Doug "and Angelina's" total domination of the game. Then the end came as a bit of an anti-climax. Angelina wasn't as excited about winning as Doug had anticipated.

After the game, Kai was invited to sing and play a song he was going to perform for a contest sponsored by a young artists' association. The performance needed a little more practice, but Kai was making progress, and Jason was reasonably confident that it would be ready in time. It felt good just to watch Kai perform, and then receive an enthusiastic response from his audience. To Jason's surprise, Kai turned to his audience without being reminded, and took a deep, theatrical bow.

Over Veronika's polite protests that they were guests, Vytautas and Birutė insisted on helping with the cleanup. With plenty of able hands, it went quickly and cheerfully, then it was time for final good-byes.

The twilight as they stepped outside was very pretty, and Birutė expressed a desire to take a slight detour along a tree-lined canal nearby that she suspected would be picturesque in the pink light. Jason volunteered to walk them back to their apartment in the interest of long good-byes, while Veronika stayed behind to get Kaarina to bed.

Doug volunteered to go with them. Jason thought that a bit odd because he didn't think that Doug was particularly attached to Vytautas and Birutė, but apparently he was in a sociable mood.

And so it seemed until after the last good-byes. Doug headed back towards the canal without a word. Jason followed.

Doug stopped at the canal and silently looked down its tree-lined length for a long time. Jason felt uncomfortable without knowing why.

"Seems like everyone's had a good time the last few days," Doug said at last.

Jason felt relieved, and wondered why he had ever felt uncomfortable. "Yeah," he answered. "It's good to have time for family and friends."

Doug turned to him and gave him a slightly puzzled look, as if Jason had said something odd. "It's good to have money for family and friends."

Jason smiled back at him. "I appreciate your generosity. I know you go through hell to earn your money."

Doug looked frustrated and shook his head. "You're missing the point. This is why I go through hell; so that I can afford to be generous with my family and provide for them whatever they need."

He gave Jason an austere look. "It's a father's responsibility to provide for his family."

Jason nodded in agreement.

"That means providing abundance, not hand-me-downs. Giving them what will make them happy," added Doug.

Now it was Jason's turn to look puzzled. "What will make them happy?"

"Always having enough. Having what they really want," answered Doug.

Something struck Jason odd about Doug's point-of-view. It didn't seem to fit the broader context. "Doug...having every material thing her heart desired didn't make mom happy, did it?" he asked slowly.

Doug seemed slightly startled by the unexpected remark, but said nothing. He recovered and resumed giving Jason a stern look.

Jason looked back with no emotion other than concern, in no hurry to say any more. He had a feeling that Doug needed some time for the truth to sink in. Finally, cocking his head slightly, he asked: "Brother, do you think you need to buy approval from those you love? Is that why you have difficulty setting limits for Angelina?"

A brief flash of anger crossed Doug's face, but he recovered almost instantly. He didn't answer.

For the first time in his life, Jason did not feel the urge to justify himself to his brother. For the first time in his life, he was certain about something, and didn't feel a need to give reasons or grovel for approval. He patiently waited for the truth to sink in, then asked: "Do you think that will work?"

He let many seconds pass, soaking in his brother's glare with an eerie sense of tranquility...then feeling something welling up from deep in his chest...that after a while he recognized as a warm glow of compassion.

"Brother," he said slowly, "that didn't work with Aimée, did it?"

Doug began trembling, at first barely noticeably, but soon alarmingly.

Jason approached him slowly, not sure how Doug would react. Doug didn't respond until Jason was well within arm's reach, whereupon he grabbed Jason roughly and pulled into a suffocating squeeze.

Jason waited patiently for him to recover. Once he had enough control, the crying and shaking disappeared with eerie suddenness. "But I don't know what I'm supposed to do," he said in an almost pleading voice. "Barbara's dead and Aimée hates me. Angelina's the only one I have left." Suddenly he lost control again and started crying, pulling Jason close enough to cry right into his cheek. "I don't know what I did wrong...or didn't do..."

Jason waited a few seconds, then whispered: "I don't know what happened either. But I am fairly certain you will get better results giving her your time and attention instead of stuff."

Jason waited patiently for Doug to recover, which once he did, he did quite abruptly, as if he'd never broken down and cried. In a few more moments, the last of his emotions were banished to the dark recesses of his psyche.

Jason grabbed Doug's forearms and faintly smiled. "I don't like seeing you get hurt. I want you to be happy. I love you because you're my brother." This time he didn't feel quite as numb and empty as he did the last time he said something along these lines.

Somewhere, deep in Jason's mind, new insights about his brother were starting to take shape. At this moment he couldn't have explained just what they were; it would take some more time before he could consciously articulate them.

He decided to set those thoughts aside for the moment to turn his attention to a more pressing issue. Right then and there, Jason made a promise to himself: he would put his family first in his life and ignore all distractions and social pressure to put his priorities elsewhere. And he would actively teach his children to do the same. He wasn't sure exactly what this commitment entailed, but he'd take the first steps and figure out the rest.

Review

If Doug had lived in the past, during a troubled time of poverty and danger, then his value as a provider and protector would be more valued than it is in the relatively safe and comfortable time and place he does live. Instead, like many men, he's considered expendable and replaceable in both the work environment and at home. Jason has the same problem, but he's starting to realize that something is wrong and he's determined to do something about it.

It's not that providing and protecting aren't needed; they are. They're just not valued as much as they should be.

And even to the extent they ever have been valued, that's not the same thing as love. Someone loves you if your presence brings happiness, and your absence brings fear and a sense of loss. If your absence is the default state of affairs, is considered normal and expected, and substitutes for your presence are bought from 3rd-parties, then you are not loved. It's probably at the heart of why the influential conservative figure mentioned in the introduction to this book has no idea what value or benefits dads provide to their families aside from a paycheck.

Doug's problems start at work: he puts in a lot of overtime trying to placate his unhappy bosses. To them, he's a cost-center they'd rather do without if they could. He's only tolerated, not appreciated.

He tries to compensate for not spending enough time with his family by buying unearned gifts for his daughters. He doesn't really believe that all the children going to someone else's party need to have gifts or they will feel left out; he's simply rationalizing his habit of trying to use gifts to buy love and approval.

For various reasons including growing bored with them or taking them for granted, gifts and favors tend not to have the effect the giver had in mind. That's not to say not to do favors, but it is to say that they're not enough to buy you love, loyalty, or respect. Unfortunately, they're also not enough to buy happiness. Have you ever met any "poor little rich kids" who have every material need taken care of, but they're bored and desperately unhappy?

Happiness is not strictly a function of our experiences, but rather a function of the meaning that we assign to them.

What will contribute more to your relationship with your kids, and their happiness, is sharing your time, attention, and cheerful, playful mood with them. Obviously it helps if you're not tied up with too much overtime at work; in that case, the problem is, at least in part, your relationship with your bosses at work. It's a similar situation to the one at home: the benefits you provide your bosses at work are a necessary, but not sufficient, condition for having a good relationship with them. I'm working on a book to cover that problem too.

In the mean time, to the extent that you have any spare time at all, allocate a generous portion of it to playing with your children, with or without toys, and give your wife attention, with or without perks like fancy vacations or bought commercial entertainment. When in doubt, keep things simple. Then they associate the good times and happy feelings with you personally, instead of to someone or something else.

The feeling of security when you play the role of leader and protector is another good feeling for your family members to be able to associate to you.

Does it often feel awkward to talk about personal matters?

A buddy of mine was telling me all about his concerns about his sons. We talked at length, but before we concluded the conversation, I asked him why he didn't talk to his sons about it instead of just worrying.

"Oh, I could never do that!" he told me.

Most men find it difficult to talk about matters that are personal, or that are laden with emotions. The problem is the male taboo on vulnerability. It's probably hardwired in our brains, and then re-enforced by our experiences in life. You've probably never been a sympathy figure. Your mistakes are the subject of ridicule, not compassion, and any weaknesses you reveal are eagerly exploited. You are constantly scrutinized for any flaws, which is why you're so self-conscious about so many matters.

It's why you can't ask for directions. It's why you don't tell the doctor about that pain you had in your chest, which is a major reason men don't live as long as women do.

It's why most men can't dance, or talk about their feelings.

There's been a movement among some men to embrace vulnerability. I understand their feelings, but I think it's not going to work out as they hope, because nobody's going to overturn billions of years of evolution by simply declaring "men's liberation," or "equality with women."

Here's a better strategy which won't bring trouble down on your head: become aware of why you are reluctant to disclose vulnerabilities, and then assess whether your taboo against vulnerability is actually serving you, or not. Think in terms of costs and benefits. What happens is that men get into such a habit of hiding vulnerabilities that they don't do any cost-benefit analysis; it's just an unconscious, unthinking reflex.

Not disclosing that pain in your chest to your doctor might kill you, which is too big of a price to pay for your reputation as a bullet-proof stud. Ending up trapped in a blizzard or a heatwave out in the middle of proverbial nowhere, because you wouldn't ask for directions of a stranger who won't even remember you five minutes later is another cost that's outsized compared to the imaginary benefit. Similarly, not being able to talk frankly with your son if you think he might have some dangerously bad habits, or if you think he might be depressed, will also come at a cost you wouldn't be willing to pay if you thought the matter through.

More generally, you want your reasoning, logical, problem-solving part of your brain to be able to over-ride your emotions, impulses, habits, and instincts any time they are not serving your best interests. That's going to the next level, from manhood to Übermenschlicheit.

One problem solved

"We'll be ready to go in about 15 minutes," Birutė informed Jason after opening the door to Doug's house.

Jason expected to see a struggle to get the kids ready to go in the car. Instead, it was fairly quiet, except for Angelina quietly chanting a vulgar insult aimed at Birutė. Jason peaked into the living room to see Angelina sitting in one corner, and Kai in another one. Birutė motioned him to the kitchen so they could talk about it.

"Angelina tossed the game pieces after we didn't play her way. Then Kai started whining about her spoiling the game, and didn't stop after being warned. So, they both got sent to the corner," she explained.

"How did you get Angelina to stay in the corner?" asked Jason, amazed.

Birutė smirked. "As if it were the first time. Now it's getting relatively easy. The first few times were a struggle. She put up quite a fight. It's a good thing we're having this battle now as I wouldn't be able to handle her if she were much bigger. In that case, I think we'd have to get her father involved. Not that we shouldn't anyway for both their sakes.

"However...eventually she realized that it's useless to resist.

"I set the timer for her time-out. If she leaves the corner before I come to get her, I escort her back and reset the timer. After a while, she noticed the pattern and realized it was in her own interest to comply."

"Wow, so much effort just to get her to submit to consequences," said Jason. "It's a good thing you're the one getting her broken in. I'm not sure Veronika would have the patience."

Birutė shrugged casually as if it were no big deal. "It's worth the effort. For one thing, training her to accept the consequences has been its own lesson in self-control. I think in the next few weeks you'll notice a lot of progress in being able to control her own behavior, often with just a warning."

"I've already noticed," said Jason. "Usually she complies on the first or second strike. But what about her taunting you like that?" He was referring to the chanting.

"Well, children need to show some respect for the adults who take care of them," answered Birutė. "But as it stands, she's already sitting in the corner, and besides, she's trying to control my behavior with a provocation. That's why in this situation it's best to ignore it. She needs to learn that she can't push my buttons like she did her mother's. I am totally in control. She can not alter my mood or my behavior."

Jason nodded. "That's one of the keys, isn't it?"

"That's right," answered Birutė. "Not only does it prevent the situation from getting out of control, but there's no better way to teach emotional self-control than by example."

Birutė excused herself and made a quick run through the house to double-check that everything was in order, then fetched her own jacket, before the timer went off. She then sat next to Angelina, and then they had a short chat about what happened and how the other players might have felt about the situation. Angelina gave a huffy promise to be a good sport next time, but then melted into Birutė's arms as they reconciled. Birutė looked up to notice Jason peaking through the doorway in amazement. She grinned and winked at him.

Then she went over to release Kai, and had a short chat with him. He resolved to control his disappointment next time, and got a hug.

Next, Angelina and Kai both got a hug and a kiss from Jason. It gave him a warm, pleasurable feeling. He hoped they got the same from him.

Angelina and Kai both got on their jackets and shoes without much fuss. The four of them left Doug's house, locking the door behind themselves, and got into the car. Birutė helped Angelina get into her seat and secure her belt, while Jason helped Kai. Then Jason opened the front passenger seat for Birutė, waited for her to be seated, and closed the door for her. Finally, he went around the car, got into the driver's seat, and they were off.

Birutė was dropped off at her apartment. Despite a recent time-out, Angelina waved to Birutė and seemed sad to part company.

Just a few more blocks and they were at Jason and Kai's home. Angelina and Kai spent days at Doug's house because the fisherman's cottage would have been a tight fit, and having them at Doug's place during the day took some pressure off of Veronika. Doug's house was also close to Angelina's school, which would be starting shortly. Kai was old enough not to need constant attention, but his mother appreciated not having to choose between neglecting him and focusing her attention on the toddler and house chores.

Because Doug tended to work late, Jason picked Angelina up along with Kai and Birutė and took her home with him. The plan was that Doug would pick her up at Jason's place if he got home at a reasonable hour, but if he were too late, then at least she'd be safe and taken care of.

The all-nighters were getting more frequent. Jason didn't mind, because he thought he had a family duty to take care of his niece, but he found it troubling that Doug was spending so much time at work. He suspected that if whatever Barbara had warned him about didn't end Doug's career, his own downward spiral of failing health, unresolved feelings, and lack of control over his life would.

Jason unlocked the door to the old fisherman's cottage and let the kids go in first. Angelina raced towards the kitchen, but he had a feeling she wasn't stopping there. Kai darted off in the direction of the bedroom. Upon entering himself, he just caught a glimpse of Veronika exiting the tiny dining nook. A steaming covered bowl of something was sitting on the dining table. He suspected that dinner was ready, but the table wasn't set.

He heard what sounded like the television in the distance.

Angelina had been told numerous times not to turn the television on without permission. There was some progress as far as at least she usually turned it off again when given direct instructions to do so. The problem was that he or Veronika always had to ask. Angelina still wasn't proactively obeying the standing order not to turn on the television.

He thought about what Vytautas would say about this situation.

"Nature abhors a vacuum." What should Angelina be doing instead of watching television? He looked at the table as Veronika re-entered with a stack of dishes, looking flustered.

His face lit up with pleasure to see her again after work. She started mumbling apologies. "Herbert's daughter came over and I had to be polite and then I lost track of time and dinner got off to a late start and..."

Jason's heart melted. He realized that his wife must have been overwhelmed with demands on her attention. He pulled her close and kissed her, then motioned for her to put down the dishes. "I have an idea," he said. "Set the dishes down; this is a blessing in disguise."

Veronika followed Jason but stopped to take care of another item for the table. Jason came back with Angelina, who was looking miffed but under control.

"What we need is place settings around the table," he told her. "Can you do that?"

"Why do I have to set the table?" she whined.

"So that we're ready to eat," answered Veronika casually. She understood what Jason was up to and apparently approved. She went to fetch Kai to help.

Jason was amazed that despite the protest, Angelina complied. In fact, she took charge of the operation, and made sure Kai was complying too.

"All of us help each other, because we're a family," commented Jason. "I go out to earn wages to pay for our rent and meals. Auntie takes care of us and our home. You and Kai help get the table ready for supper."

"I really appreciate your help setting the table. I see that you set them neatly," he said after she finished. He remembered to praise the action, not the child.

Angelina exhaled a bit forcefully, but that was the worst of it until later, during the meal.

"That's my sippy-cup!" she screamed as she jerked it out of Kai's hands. Kai started protesting loudly on his own part.

Jason caught himself getting ready to plead with Angelina, but instead heard himself saying in a calm but clear, deep voice: "Strike one."

Veronika looked relieved that Jason was taking the initiative.

"That's not fair; it's my sippy cup, why can't I have it?" she demanded.

"That's not how you ask for it. Strike two," said Jason.

Angelina threw down the cup and started crying.

"Strike three, you're out," Jason said. He got up to escort Angelina to her time-out spot, but she withdrew from the table on her own.

Veronika muttered something about how many more fights like this one they'd have on their hands. But then she looked pleasantly surprised when Angelina came back a few minutes later, calm. There was no total, lingering melt-down this time. That was unexpected.

Maybe the method was working.

Later, Jason negotiated an understanding on the sippy-cup issue. It caught both Jason and Veronika totally off-guard that she would claim it much less feel she still needed one. Apparently, her father had unthinkingly donated it without first obtaining his daughter's buy-in. This was a skirmish that didn't have to happen.

Jason considered what Vytautas had said about empathizing with the child's point of view. Children feel very powerless, and crave control over their lives. Angelina wasn't looking for a fight; she was just acting on instinct to defend her property rights.

After dinner, Angelina agreed to help take dirty dishes to the kitchen counter. Kai had already disappeared somewhere.

Jason focused on turning the plan into a routine. Veronika was on-board because it reminded her of the way that she had a few chores from the time she was a little younger than Angelina, and she realized she needed the help.

Jason hoped Veronika's patience with Angelina would not run out. Both of them were stubborn. But as the routine started developing, and Angelina's impulsiveness became possible to control most of the time, Jason started feeling confident in his ability to know how to establish a routine and respond to problems. It wasn't just knowing specific words to say or rules to follow; he was starting to develop an intuition.

○ ○ ○

One day after dinner, he went fishing for compliments from Veronika. "Angelina is shaping up. This new system of discipline is working," he said.

"Hmm," was her only reply. After a long pause, she asked: "What about our son?"

"Huh? Kai? What about him?" asked Jason, wondering what she was getting at. Kai had never acted up as much as Angelina.

Veronika shot him a challenging look. "Where is he?"

Jason thought for a moment, then realized what the problem was. Kai was watching television with Herbert again.

Jason looked at her sheepishly. "I suppose I'd better start organizing better uses for his time too." He paused briefly as he considered the matter. "But everything that Vytautas and Birutė taught us is about how to get kids to stop doing what you don't want them to do. They didn't say much about motivating kids to do what you do want them to do. Vytautas specifically said that was a conversation for another time."

"Well, then, you'd better ask them how next time they're over for supper!" said Veronika.

Jason sighed, and then smiled.

Review

Birutė's calm emotions, her empathy, and her rapport-building skills are how she can handle children who previously had been hard to handle.

Angelina sometimes misbehaves and resists orders, but once she puts her mind to something, it gets done. Her strong will is useful when it's channeled in the right direction. Kai, on the other hand, is easier to keep out of trouble, but his passive, introverted personality, exacerbated by passive-attention activities, makes him more challenging to motivate.

One problem solved

Calm, rational, in-charge dads make more resourceful men

People who over-react emotionally to mundane problems are said to be "neurotic." If you don't already have an intuitive sense of what that means, it's the behavior patterns that were often portrayed by the actor Woody Allen when he was playing a low-status character. It was also portrayed by the actor Tony Randall when he was playing the character Felix Unger in "The Odd Couple" (actually, both lead characters were very neurotic, but audiences seem to notice it more in Felix than in Oscar because Oscar's angry outbursts are considered more "manly" than Felix's "upset" outbursts).

The emotional over-reactions are part of a bigger pattern of ham-fisted ways of evading problems instead of resolving them. For example, the character Felix is prone to exaggerating the effects of his own real or imagined health problems so that other people are supposed to feel sorry for him and accommodate him. Neurotics resort to these behaviors when they're overwhelmed with a problem that's too big for their level of psychological maturity. If the behavior helps evade the problem once, it's likely to be tried again when the problem re-occurs, and from there it turns into a habit. It usually starts in childhood, when their parents fail to provide safety and mentorship, and model the maladaptive evasion themselves.

One common problem that triggers neurotic reactions is low social status. People who have low social status constantly feel like they're on the defensive. The relationship between neurosis and social status exhibits quite a bit of "reflexivity" (that is, if A causes B, B causes A): if you behave neurotically, people will unconsciously assume that you're a low-status character and treat you accordingly. On the other hand, if people think of you as being low-status and treat you disrespectfully, but you DON'T feel needy for their approval and DON'T react emotionally to their little digs and put-downs, you're invalidating their assumptions about you, and they'll start to doubt themselves. If you hold your ground, you'll wear down their resolve to put you in your place.

By the way, propensity for neurosis inversely correlates to testosterone levels: men with high testosterone levels tend to be less neurotic.

I'm not aware of any exact antonym for neurotic; the closest I can come up with is "imperturbable". The more you can train yourself to stay calm and rational when mundane child-rearing problems come up, the more imperturbable you'll become.

Get into the habit of noticing your own emotional reactions to things. Kid acts up really bad. Do you get angry or upset? Or do you stay calm and in-control? If you do catch yourself reacting emotionally, ask yourself if the emotion is helping the situation or making it worse. Remember, strong emotions override your "higher self" that makes choices and comes up with creative solutions to problems: they channel your behavior into primitive "reptilian" behaviors like "fight," "flight," and "freeze." Think about that carefully: when you get angry with a child, your body and mind are getting ready a physical fight. That's how child-abuse happens. Getting into "flight" mode means being a wimp who is likely to try appeasing increasingly bratty kids. Getting into "freeze" mode means being a passive dad who passes the buck to mom.

If you catch yourself reacting to your kids with negative emotions, stop, realize it's interfering with your ability to make a conscious, rational choice regarding how you respond, then let go of the negative emotion as quickly as possible with a deep breath and a sigh. The more you do this, the more imperturbable you'll become generally.

Personally, I've benefited from mindfulness training. I make a point of paying attention to whom I'm engaging, what's happening, and how I'm responding, to put my attention back where it matters, and by the same token starve out unhelpful, distracting mental chatter that would interfere with my ability to maintain a calm, rational, alert state-of-mind.

Now imagine that it's the boss at work who's acting up. How do you respond to him? Anger/fight? You'll get fired. Fear/flight? He'll think you're a wimp, and lose whatever respect for you he ever had, if any. Fear/freeze? You'll fail to deal with the problem, it will escalate, and you'll get fired.

If you stay calm and rational, he's more likely to retain or develop some respect for you, and at worst, you'll at least maintain the ability to respond rationally and creatively.

Same goes with wives.

Imperturbability is a blessing you can pass on to your own children: the better you manage your own emotions, the better they'll tend to manage theirs.

This advice is probably some of the best you'll ever get for such a small price.

Good baseline mood and good self-esteem prevent a lot of trouble

When I was a lad, there were a lot of young people getting into trouble with drugs and promiscuous sex. As I write this, vice is still a temptation, but now there is additionally an epidemic of political radicalism.

It can run the gamut from shrieking "cry-bullies" who rack up tremendous amounts of debt in college both on their own account as well as their parents' while they play political activist (instead of, say, getting marketable skills), to thugs on the streets of Portland, Oregon, who beat up Andy Ngô for being gay, of-color, and conservative.

It is now everywhere, not just Portland. The problem is happening in the heartland of the USA as well as throughout Europe, even in small towns. Children and adolescents are radicalized in schools (both public and private nowadays), in college, in corrupted religious organizations, and through the world-wide-web which reaches pretty much everywhere now.

By all means, protect your kids from bad influences; I'll say that over and over again. Kids are exposed to problems before they have enough experience and maturity to know how to deal with them.

But first of all, you can't always be around them; you have a living to make. Second, the older they get, the more they have to be on their own anyway. If nothing else, eventually you'll be dead and gone. So you have to get them ready to protect themselves from bad influences.

Sinister characters have less influence over kids with good self-esteem. The reason is that kids with good esteem are less needy for approval. The political radicalization process, for example, happens when kids are too needy for approval from radical teachers, or teachers teaching from radicalizing textbooks. Some vices are the result of being too needy for approval from the "cool kids".

Most vices are the result of looking for a quick way to improve a mood. Someone who is already in a good mood doesn't need that. Kids who are generally content with life are less likely to be tempted by vice-pushers. That includes teachers and college professors offering purely psychological rewards like approval. Happy kids who "feel comfortable in their own skin" aren't needy for approval in the first place. They can afford to know their own mind and stand their own ground.

New directions

It had been a busy Saturday morning.

First, it was jiu-jitsu for physical and mental training.

Kai was in another corner of the gym, with other youngsters. Jason's ears were finely-tuned to any reprimands that might tip him off to any goofing-off Kai might be involved with. Thankfully the old instructor seemed to have a good rapport with the kids.

It was Jason who was constantly in trouble. He was out-of-shape and a newbie. It felt humiliating to watch even elderly students perform better than himself. After the lesson, he reminded himself that anything worth learning had to require some effort. Once he was over the learning curve, he'd stop feeling so self-conscious.

Jason recalled one of the reasons he was here: the mob attack at the shopping mall. The memory triggered a surge of determination on his part. He wanted to make sure he could at least offer resistance the next time his family members were threatened.

After class, Jason & Kai rushed to change into street clothes, then breezed out the door. The mini-mall where the gym was located also accommodated a Chinese deli. Jason had peaked in a few times for a look. There was soy-sauce chicken, barbecue pork, onion daufu braised in sweetened soy sauce, lightly steamed vegetables, braised green jackfruit with sweetened soy-sauce and garlic, chow mien with vegetables, and similar fare, some of it familiar, some novel. There were also a few grocery items to compliment the deli items, like boxes of loose green jasmine tea. For dessert, fried Chinese "doughnuts" made out of sticky rice flour sprinkled with sesame seeds and filled with red bean paste, or silken daufu accompanied by ginger-infused syrup, though truth be told, Jason would rather pick up some treats from the tiny Chinese bakery next door, whose shelves were full of exquisite Hong-Kong-style baked, filled rolls and pastries. His mouth watered at the thought of buying a few items for lunch and, say, afternoon tea, but he was under the impression that there were leftovers to be taken care of. On a whim, he motioned to Kai to follow him into the bakery, where they bought one pastry to divide into one small bite for each family member. Jason slipped Kai some paper cash to pay for the item, then encouraged him to hand it over to the teenager behind the counter and collect and count their change.

Next, they had to rush to another part of town for Kai's audition with the Young Artist's Association. Maybe after their next lesson they'd pick up a full meal, Jason thought as he and Kai scrambled into the car.

The scene of the auditions was chaotic. There were lots of tables set up, but it wasn't clear which one they needed to register at. Even the staff at the tables didn't know where to send them. It took several false starts before they finally found a table with a registrar who had their names on the list.

They were a few minutes late as they got to the performance hall. Jason was worried that they would create a disturbance when they entered, but in fact, the people coming and going, not to mention talking right during the performances, created enough distraction that their entrance went un-noticed.

Unfortunately, Jason had no idea if Kai's name had already been called. There were no programs. He worried that they would get to the end of the performance, and Kai had already missed his chance. There was no way of knowing until and unless Kai's name was called.

Most of the parents were leaving the performance hall as soon as their children were done auditioning, so that by the time Kai's name was called, just past the mid-point of the auditions, there was only a small audience left. After Kai was done, Jason thought it best to stay for the rest of the performances, so that the remaining performers would have as much audience as possible.

Having seen all but the first few acts, Jason thought he had a pretty good idea how Kai's performance compared to the rest. Jason didn't want to judge harshly, but it looked pretty obvious that most of them hadn't been sufficiently rehearsed. Performers forgot their lines, collided with each other while dancing or acting, and several were missing their music. Some of the acts, like lip-synching, didn't seem to require much skill. Jason estimated that Kai was comfortably within the top three performers. Top ten were going to perform later in the evening, so it seemed like he was a shoo-in.

Jason wondered what the next step in the process would be. It seemed like a bad idea to have scheduled the audition and the performance the same day; he didn't think the sponsors were sufficiently well-organized to promptly notify the winners. Given that most of the performers and their parents had already left the premises, someone would have to make a lot of phone calls.

Jason and Kai headed home for a late lunch. Veronica had set out some leftover rolls, leftover meat scraps, greens, cheese, home-made mayonnaise, and smokey-hot-sweet German mustard for making rustic sandwiches.

"Well, what's the word?" she asked.

"About what, Kai's performance?" asked Jason. "He did a good job."

"Well, then, is he going to perform this evening?" she asked, sounding a little worried.

"I assume so, but I don't know for sure," said Jason. "There were no announcements afterwards, and there was no one available to ask."

"You must have overlooked something," she said in a scolding tone of voice. "Of course they would have to have the result ready; otherwise there's not enough time for the performers to get ready."

Jason was about to defend himself, but Veronika abruptly left the room. Jason assumed that the conversation wasn't over so followed her into the bedroom, where he found her staring at her cell phone. She looked up a number, dialed it, and handed it to Jason, informing him that this was her contact for the Association.

The phone rang a few times, then a woman's voice answered.

"Hello, ah, this is Kai Olson's dad. My wife and I were wondering if our son will be performing this evening and..."

"Oh no!" the voice interrupted. "No boys!". She said it in a tone of voice that communicated unmistakable disgust, as if he had just committed some horrifying social faux pas.

"Uh. OK," said Jason, suddenly flustered. "Thank you. Sorry to trouble you."

Jason ended the call and looked at Veronika's anxious face.

"No?" she guessed.

"Uh, yeah, no," said Jason. After collecting his thoughts for a moment, he said: "Maybe since we don't have plans for this evening, we'll play a game instead."

Veronika suddenly looked more relaxed. Apparently she had been more worried about being ready than actually winning. "Well, next year we'll just have to try harder," she said. She then left the room to go check on Kaarina.

Jason stood there, eyes defocused. He knew that he felt bad, but it didn't make sense to him why he felt that way. Winning a spot in the show wouldn't have conferred any real benefit. Did he need strangers to validate Kai's worth? Surely not.

As for trying harder, he had a feeling that wouldn't help. He felt discouraged. Maybe it wasn't worth the effort to audition next year.

He began to wonder how Kai would feel about it. He'd find out imminently, as he had to inform Kai that he would not be performing later in the evening.

He found Kai eating at one of Herbert's little folding TV trays. Horrible bachelor habit, but the TV wasn't on, Herbert having already eaten and fallen asleep in his chair. He was snoring heavily, which meant he could be safely ignored as he wouldn't wake easily.

"Hey, Bud!" Jason began, to get his son's attention. Kai looked up, but Jason got down on his level. He didn't feel comfortable talking down to him.

Jason looked Kai in the eye. "Looks like we won't need to go to the performance this evening. We can stay home and play a game instead."

Kai suddenly looked serious. "They don't want me to play in the performance?" he asked. Jason sensed disappointment.

He sighed. "They want someone else instead." Then he tried to look more cheerful, and added: "But I wouldn't worry about that. You played great."

Kai had nothing to say. He broke eye contact, his face drifting down, his eyes defocused.

"Listen, Bud, finish up your lunch, and then we can have a little piece of the pastry we brought back from the bakery. After that, you can help me take care of the car," said Jason enthusiastically.

Kai looked back up into his father's eyes. He seemed interested. It was more likely the offer of working on the car than the pastry; he liked helping dad. And Jason would make it fun. After doing some maintenance, they'd wash it, and there would probably be some action with the hose that would trigger some laughs.

Jason smiled at Kai, gave him a wink, and then went to the kitchenette to assemble his own lunch.

That evening, after supper, there was no game. Not a big deal, since they'd already played a game yesterday on their regular game night. Instead, somehow, spontaneously, a roughhousing session broke out. Jason didn't feel as if he had any idea what he was doing, but Kai didn't know any better. Even Kaarina, for her part, was squealing with excitement as she watched the action. Herbert grinned from his recliner. Veronika sat slowly rocking in her rocking chair, with a dreamy look on her face, watching.

Sunday evening was the occasion for another big family-and-friends dinner. This time Doug brought some sashimi, grilled marinated eel, various marinated vegetables, teriyaki mushrooms, daikon sprouts, nori sheets, daufu pockets for making inarizushi, a thermos containing miso-shiru, and some previously steamed but now chilled spinach and sesame-dressing for making goma-ae. Veronika contributed sushi rice and a "jiggly" Japanese-style cheesecake, both made in the multipot. Because it had been steamed instead of baked, the cheesecake came out with a pale, off-white dome instead of the usual brown, which struck Jason as unappetizing for failing to conform to his expectations, but he knew it would taste about the same as if it had come out of an oven the traditional way.

Guests were invited to hand-roll their own sushi cones from whichever ingredients they wanted. Jason worried that the fare might be a little exotic for Herbert, but it turned out that while he had only ever had sushi a few times in his life, the occasion was back when he was flown to Japan for emergency repair-work, and the food brought back reminiscences he was delighted to share.

The atmosphere was informal, and instead of one conversation, there were three going on. Angelina and Kai were having one conversation while playing card games, Veronika and Birutė were having another with Herbert in his corner of the room as Veronika held Kaarina, and a third among Doug, Vytautas, and Jason.

Jason started the conversation, but he had a feeling that Doug might also take an interest. Doug always pushed himself—and increasingly these days, Jason too—to perform.

"So to get a behavior to stop, you assign consequences. I understand that part," said Jason. "What about getting good behavior to start? Like doing homework or chores? Rewards?"

"Yes, but there's a catch," said Vytautas. "It's not a completely symmetric situation. To get bad behavior to stop, you have to be ready to assign consequences each and every time that a direct order is disobeyed. But to get good behavior to start, you can't reward it every time."

"Eh?" said Doug, surprised. "That doesn't sound very fair."

"I've heard a rumor that life isn't fair," said Vytautas with a twinkle in his eye. "Think about what's going on. If you tie the target behavior to the reward, then it's a transaction. What do you suppose happens to the desired behavior if the reward isn't available or worse, the child loses interest in the reward?"

Doug raised an eyebrow as he considered. "You could raise the stakes, but I see where that is going."

"In fact, you'd have to raise the stakes," said Vytautas. "We're all dopamine addicts. And like with any addition, over time it takes more and more of the drug to achieve pleasure. Until one day it's out of reach, and we lose our ability to feel pleasure and motivation."

"That's depression, isn't it?" asked Doug.

"It is!" answered Vytautas. "Over-use of rewards that are too easy to get, and too much stimulation generally, are why so many young people are lacking any joie de vivre anymore.

"The only point in doing anything is for real rewards. The kind you get after picking yourself back up off the ground and trying again and again until you get it right. The only point of using artificial rewards at all is as a crutch when real rewards are a little too distant and a little too abstract for a child's perspectives."

"Wait a minute, am I supposed to give rewards, or not?" asked Doug.

"You give a little reward only every now and then, unexpectedly, and only for best work," answered Vytautas. "It might sound counter-intuitive, but think about how gambling works. Ironically, if the rewards were too easy to get, or too predictable, gamblers wouldn't get addicted."

Doug looked thoughtful. "If rewards are too easy to get, it cheapens them."

"By the same token, if expectations are too low, children—or for that matter, adults too—get bored," said Vytautas. "In fact, that's what a lot of performance training is about: staying in the zone. Not too easy, or else bored. Not too hard, or else overwhelmed and stressed. The 'zone' is where you have a comfortable level of challenge just above whatever your level of mastery is."

"That sounds like sports training," said Doug.

"Same concept applied to any sort of training," said Vytautas. "A lot of problems happen as the result of either over-training or under-training. If a child is struggling with a skill, then the pace is probably too fast. If a child shows obvious signs of boredom, the pace is probably too slow."

"Then why are teachers fanatical about keeping all the students at the same pace?" asked Doug. "It seems as though that should guarantee a disaster for students at both ends of the curve."

"What makes you think it's not?" asked Vytautas. "It's the factory-farming model applied to humans, who are considerably more variable than modern, highly-inbred crops. It's a legacy holdover from way back when books were written by hand, and the teachers were literally reading the book to the whole class for lack of each student having a copy. So at first, they had to keep them synchronized. Then the teachers became obsessed with mandating equality as an end in itself."

"Angelina does seem bored in school," said Doug. "But luckily she still has a pretty good rapport with her teachers."

Doug finished off the last of one of his rolls.

"She gets plenty of praise and encouragement from them," he continued after swallowing. "But to tell the truth, she's a lot more eager to please them than me. I can't get her to do anything!"

Angelina must have overheard what her dad said. She turned away from her game and stuck her tongue out at him.

Doug must have noticed out the corner of his eye. He grinned, then stood up, walked towards the back door carrying his plate of food, then motioned for Jason and Vytautas to follow him as he headed out to the back porch. Doug took one of the wicker chairs set there for enjoying summer evenings, Vytautas took the one next to Doug's, and Jason a third one facing the other two.

"Now then, as we were saying..." started Doug.

"Your daughter is more eager to please the teachers than you," said Vytautas.

Doug rubbed his bearded chin and looked thoughtful. "Not surprising, I suppose. She has to work for their approval. She knows I love her unconditionally."

"Right," said Vytautas. "A common pattern."

"So...maybe that's just the way it has to be," said Doug. "Someone else has to teach your kids and get them to perform."

Vytautas raised his eyebrows. "Hold on there. I think you might be over-estimating someone else's importance in the scheme of things, and under-estimating your own."

"How so?" asked Doug.

"You just said a few minutes ago that Angelina gets plenty of praise from her teachers," said Vytautas. "Is that really helpful? And I wonder if 'plenty' is actually too much."

"What do you mean?" asked Doug. "Isn't that how you encourage kids?"

"Perhaps, but praise is apt to backfire," said Vytautas.

Doug looked concerned. "Elaborate please."

"Well, first of all, what kinds of praise do they give her?" asked Vytautas. "Do they tell her what a good girl she is? How smart she is?"

Doug nodded. "Yeah, that would be typical."

"It would be better if they praised what she does, not what she is," said Vytautas. "And even that, only occasionally, and only for her best work."

"The problem with labels is that they distort thinking," he continued. "Your daughter can't *be* good. It's not a personal attribute. It's not something she is; it's something she does. Or doesn't do. In which case a girl who thinks she's good may not realize when what she's doing is naughty."

Doug chuckled. "Yeah, that would be my little Angelina." Then he looked serious. "But do you really think labels are necessarily harmful? For example, if someone thinks of himself as an athlete, isn't he more likely to take his training seriously?"

"Yes, that's true he is," answered Vytautas. "But it's still thinking in terms of static qualities instead of in terms of actions and behaviors. It's still causing a distortion in the way people think about things."

Vytautas took a sip of his green tea before continuing.

"Suppose that your athlete also thought of himself as 'muscular' and 'fit.' Suppose those traits are a fundamental aspect of his self-image. Perhaps he is indeed genetically gifted with a well-built physique. Well then, any reason to push himself when it just comes naturally? That one day, when he just doesn't feel up to training, might he be willing to blow it off?"

Doug gave it some thought. "Maybe even more so when someone thinks of herself as being 'smart'?" he wondered aloud.

"How many 'smart kids' did you meet in college who promptly flunked out their first year?" asked Vytautas.

Doug nodded. "If they're smart, they don't need to study. In fact, they probably got good grades in high school without studying, because it was easy. So they never got into the habit."

His eyes defocused for a few seconds as he thought something over in his head. "I'm not too worried about exactly that happening to my older daughter, Aimée. I don't think she'll flunk out, anyway. More likely, never challenge herself at all. Instead, sign up for some idiotic social justice major in college, where she doesn't have to do any real work to earn all 'A's."

"Different outcome, same cause," remarked Vytautas. "If someone thinks of herself as 'smart,' the last thing she wants is for reality to invalidate her opinion of herself. So, she avoids any chance of that happening. It's a well-known phenomenon regarding children who've been praised too much.

"Notoriously, that's why Asian immigrant parents tend to take the opposite approach and downplay their children's achievements. That's one reason their children tend to go for the more prestigious majors and get higher grades and test scores."

"Hmm, but isn't there a dark side to that?" asked Doug. "Like all the suicides in Japan and Hong Kong among the students who flunk their entrance exams?"

"Not caused by withholding praise," said Vytautas. "Caused by an unrealistic expectation that every kid needs to be above-average."

"Whereas here in the States everybody gets a participation prize," said Doug.

"Not everybody!" Jason said, suddenly feeling a little hot under the collar. "Kai didn't get any recognition from the talent show judges. And I'm pretty sure that, objectively, his was one of the best acts!"

Doug didn't react. It looked like he was thinking.

"In the English-speaking countries, you continue going through the motions of auditions and tests, but assign the rewards for other reasons," remarked Vytautas.

"You know...there's some truth to that," Doug said with uncharacteristic hesitation. "When I graduated from high school, I was expecting to be named valedictorian. I had the highest GPA despite taking a heavy load of hard classes. Another boy took a lighter and easier load, but he had a GPA that was almost as high...so the school administrators called it a tie."

Doug looked down, at nothing in particular, and paused for just a moment. "Except they gave the award to him, not me. So it wasn't even a tie. Now that you mention it, I can't help thinking it was because he was the star of their lucrative foreign student program."

"So they gave you salutatorian?" asked Jason. The topic was a bit of a sore point for himself since he never even had the chance to graduate, much less with any prospect for honors.

Doug shook his head slowly. "No. They said they needed 'gender balance' and awarded it to a girl."

Doug shook his head vigorously, as if to awaken himself from a trance. "Well, then, you're right, life's not fair. Might as well get used to that."

"That's why it's important to protect self-esteem in your kids," said Vytautas. "It's dangerous to leave them too needy for approval."

"So how does a dad protect self-esteem?" asked Doug.

"It's mostly a matter of what he doesn't do. He heaps neither scorn and criticism, nor praise and adulation on their heads. And..." Vytautas hesitated before continuing, apparently for emphasis. "...he doesn't allow others to do those things either."

"How does praise damage self-esteem?" asked Doug.

"It depends on how you define self-esteem," answered Vytautas. "Most people think of it as being a matter of having a positive self-image. But that can turn into what psychologists call 'narcissism.' It's the other side of the coin from a negative self-image."

"Scylla and Charybdis," commented Doug. "What's the alternative?"

"Simple. Not having a big ego at all," answered Vytautas. "Neither feeling good about yourself, nor feeling bad about yourself. Just feeling good. Being comfortable in your own skin."

Doug looked down and sighed. "My older daughter got a lot of praise heaped on her head." He paused for a moment before continuing. "And she is indeed a remarkably self-centered young woman."

"Why do you suppose that some kids get all the praise and others get none?" asked Vytautas. "I mean, aside from life not being fair."

"Well, you have to admit..." Doug started with a big grin on his face, but then he paused. "...oh, I guess you wouldn't know, never having met her. Aimée is not only smart, she's quite attractive too, even if I do say so myself."

"Is Kai ugly?" asked Jason, feeling a little indignant.

"No, but..." Doug started, then paused briefly before adding "...he's a boy." He paused again, apparently thinking the situation through in his head. "The teachers and youth group leaders definitely favor the girls. Is that..." He hesitated again. "...sexual?"

The question didn't seem to be addressed to anyone in particular. Neither Vytautas nor Jason had an answer.

But Jason had an observation to contribute. Something that had been bugging him a long time. "Think about Barbara's friend Moriah," he said. "I wonder if that's why she dresses her son like a girl. Converted a worthless boy into a valuable girl."

Doug's face started turning red. Jason had the feeling he was fighting a strong emotion. "Moriah bragged to us once that she recruits these so-called 'uncles' to take him out and spend money on him," Doug said. The tightening of the muscles in his thick neck altered the timbre of his voice.

"There's someone else I've always had a bad feeling about," he continued. "A church youth group leader. I picked up hostile vibes the day we met. Badmouthed me behind my back. And that's when Aimée started picking up bad habits..."

"While the cat's away, the mice will play," said Vytautas softly.

"The cat was busy trying to make a living," Doug said ruefully. "That's how I paid for all those youth activities. Including some expensive retreats."

Vytautas looked like he wanted to say something, but he hesitated. Doug noticed. "Say it!" he commanded.

"Well, first of all, the whole point of those retreats was to get her away from you," Vytautas said.

Doug exhaled forcefully. "Yeah, I've come to realize that. Too late."

"Do you suspect grooming?" asked Vytautas. "I mean, in the more general American sense, not the British sense."

"What's the difference?" asked Doug. "I mean, between the two senses of the word. Not that familiar with Briticisms."

"When Brits refer to 'grooming gangs', they're referring to men who prepare teenage girls for a life of prostitution," answered Vytautas. "I assume Aimée has enough self-esteem and opportunities to stay out of that."

Doug nodded. "I didn't think you meant that."

"What I meant was in the more general American sense of when sketchy people isolate young people from their parents and habituate them to themselves and to their bad habits," said Vytautas. "Often enough, when the groomers have access to resources someone else is paying for, they'll use those to sweeten the deal."

"What do you mean?" asked Doug.

"About habituating kids to themselves, or about sweetening the deal?" asked Vytautas.

"Both," answered Doug.

"By habituation I mean that they don't notice the vices like a fish doesn't notice water. Ever hear horror stories about small children who've been discovered handling sex toys very familiarly?"

Jason noticed the muscles in his brother's neck tightening again. "Yeah, I've heard of it. Close at hand," answered Doug.

"The intention isn't necessarily to force the vice on the child..." Vytautas started.

"...but it might be," interrupted Doug. "And even if it isn't, if the vice is too familiar, there's no resistance to trying it out themselves once they realize what it is."

"...which brings me to the second part of the answer," said Vytautas. "Another groomer trick is to sponsor a lot of pleasurable activities so that the child associates the adult to fun-fun-fun."

"...which gets back to the problem of dopamine addiction," said Doug. "The kid is going to need a bigger and bigger dose of fun...while all those vices are close at hand..."

"Bingo!" said Vytautas. "But even if she got jaded from too much fun, if Aimée had that fun in someone else's company, that's who figures in her happy memories..." Vytautas said.

"...and not me," Doug concluded bitterly.

He looked pensive and moody again. Something else was bothering him. "I got put down. A lot. It wasn't just the youth group leader. Our whole bloody social circle.

"I don't know what the problem was. I make good money. Not as much as Barbara did, but I can't help that marketing is considered more valuable than programming. I tried to be a good father. Maybe I wasn't perfect. Experience is a harsh teacher: test first, lesson afterwards."

"It's unrealistic to blame yourself when other people treat you unfairly," said Vytautas gently. "You have a lot to show for yourself, and I bet that was true from a younger age than I am.

Doug smirked. "I appreciate the vote of confidence, Bud, but it's hardly a comforting thought that they would have eaten you alive even faster than me." Doug smiled, winked at Vytautas, and smacked him playfully on the arm, apparently to let

Vytautas know that it was all in good fun, and he didn't intend to put Vytautas down.

Vytautas showed no signs of taking offense or feeling hurt. Instead, he looked Doug squarely in the eye. "...and if I had been in the same social circle, they'd have to try a lot harder than that to get my goat," he said confidently.

Doug met Vytautas's eye. Vytautas had his full attention.

"It's unwise to allow one's self-esteem to depend on anyone else's approval. Especially if they have a reason to withhold it no matter what!"

"And what would that be?" asked Doug.

"To get dad out of the way, of course," answered Vytautas.

"To get unfettered access to the daughter," muttered Doug.

"Isn't that why couples where the oldest is a daughter are more likely to end up divorced?" asked Vytautas. "The trouble started shortly after Aimée hit her teens, didn't it?"

Doug nodded. Then he looked down shamefacedly. "And you think Aimée might have lost her respect for me when she noticed that nobody else respects me either."

Vytautas sighed. "I can't read her mind. But given how things turned out, that's the most likely explanation."

There was a long pause in the conversation. Doug had just violated the taboo on male vulnerability. Jason and Vytautas didn't know what to say to cheer him up.

Doug sighed. "Well, I screwed up with Aimée. But at least I still have Angelina. Maybe I'll do better with her. But I'm not quite sure what to change. I don't know what more I could have done."

"Are you open to some suggestions?" asked Vytautas.

Doug nodded.

"That social circle," said Vytautas. "They weren't your friends were they?"

Doug looked down again. "No. They were Barbara's. A fact that's all the more obvious now that she's gone."

"What fraction of the women had already rid themselves of their own husbands?" asked Vytautas.

"At least half," answered Doug. "And...ah...several of them were not just flaunting their 'freedom', but encouraging other women in the social circle to claim their own."

"That situation was always a disaster waiting to happen," said Vytautas. "A man should always have his own friends. Men who respect him and will watch his back. Your social involvement with a friendlier bunch could have displaced some with the hostile crowd."

Doug looked pained. "Yes, it would have been nice to have friends. I tried. Nascent friendships never went anywhere, and then they fizzled out."

"As for Barbara's friends, you could have displaced some of their involvement in her life with more of your own," said Vytautas.

"Well, they're not as much of a problem going forward as they used to be. They're out of my life now. But as for more involvement with Angelina, I'm still stretched thin," said Doug.

"I didn't say it would be easy," said Vytautas. "You can't avoid hard choices. But, the longer you live, the more the quality of your life will be a function of the choices you do make."

Doug looked at Vytautas for several seconds, and then he nodded slightly.

Later that evening, after everything was cleaned up and the guests departed, Jason performed his nightly bedtime story routine. It was about a family of chickens making a plan for how they were going to get past the fox.

After the story was over, and sleepy good-nights exchanged, Jason snuggled up close to Veronika. She responded by pulling Jason's hand over her belly. Jason waited eagerly.

Then there it was: a rhythmic sensation of tiny kicking legs.

The excitement of that feeling stirred up Jason's mind. He tried to relax into sleep, but thoughts about recent events kept him awake. He kept wondering what life was supposed to be. The illusions he had previously harbored had been shattered in the aftermath of his parents' divorce.

It was a mystery, and he assumed that the clues lay in his memories of his own childhood. But the more he tried to scan his memories for clues, the more he ran into obstacles. It wasn't that he couldn't remember; it was that it was becoming painful to do so.

That was the strange part. Memories he used to interpret as happy ones were now sad. Birthday parties. Playing with cousins he was now deeply estranged from for no particular reason. Holidays.

In particular, he remembered one Christmas morning—he must have just turned two—when they had a Christmas tree covered in heirloom, hand-painted glass ornaments, and underneath the tree was a big pile of boxes wrapped in colorful paper. That morning, he spent what must have been hours opening packages, and there were so many fascinating toys inside. They included some antiques that someone—probably his dad or Todd—had picked up in Nuremberg, Germany. He remembered a big, colorful tin top, and a toy accordion that really worked. It looked a lot like a real one, just scaled down. He remembered looking forward to playing with them.

But after that Christmas morning, he never did. He never even saw them again.

Unruly thoughts swirled around in his head, resisting his efforts to sort them out and make sense of them, until finally the effort left him mentally-exhausted. After his mind finally calmed down, he decided that while he would like to learn from his past, it wasn't going to give up its secrets so easily. For the moment, he just had to accept that there was nothing he could do to change the past. What he could do was to set a firm intention to make better choices for his own kids than the choices others had made for him. He still didn't know exactly what that entailed.

But he felt sure that he'd taken a step in the right direction.

New directions

Jason's story will continue with the next book!

Why do so many of Jason's relationships seem to be loaded with unpleasant surprises waiting to be sprung on him? Sign up at our website to be notified when the story continues.

Review
(and a little expansion)

Martial arts training helps kids maintain self-esteem, and it might just help them out if they get into a confrontational situation that can't be resolved without having to defend themselves.

Martial arts also helps kids control and properly channel their own aggression. Boys who train in martial arts are LESS likely to bully than boys who don't. That's probably true of girls too. This is counter-intuitive to some people, but it actually makes a lot of sense.

Dads benefit from the same training. In the increasingly dangerous times as these words are being written, it is unwise to rely on police or private security to defend yourself and those you love. It also makes good father-son or even father-daughter bonding activity, if you're lucky to have access to a teacher that has training sessions like that. Otherwise, try some family training at home.

The "no boys" incident is based on a real-life incident. It's become fairly common. Instead of complaining about unfairness, which doesn't help, encourage your kids to be self-motivated, and to be happy without needing anyone else's permission or approval.

The "passed up for valedictorian status" was also a real-life incident. That too is becoming common. In some cases, they drop academic rewards altogether, but hand out awards for reasons other than for objective accomplishments, thereby cheapening the rewards. That's why it's important to learn self-motivation. Life's not fair.

Give unpredictable, somewhat random rewards only for best performance. Don't make deals where you hand out stickers for routine performance, or offer bribes like quarters or candy for doing routine chores, because that cheapens the reward (not to mention candy rots their teeth). Otherwise, they eventually get bored with it, decide they don't need the quarter or the candy, and then refuse to perform.

It's not a good idea to praise personal qualities: "You're so smart!" Praise behavior sparingly when earned: "You worked hard on that project and did a good job."

Any activity that attracts children also attracts people who should not have access to them! Take initiative: extreme vetting!

The most common pattern of sexual predation is men going after girls, and that's what you're probably most conscious of, for good reason. Beware that same-sex predation is common in both sexes. The least common pattern is adult women going after boys, but as numerous teacher-student scandals have shown, even that's not particularly rare. Many adults assume that woman-boy relationships are harmless. They aren't if she gets pregnant and socks him with child-support, or if she gives him a venereal disease.

Sexual predation is not the only type of danger other people will put your kids in. Dads tend to have finely-tuned instincts for violence and sexual predation, but less so for less immediate dangers. There's a lot of bad judgment that other people are willing to impose on your kids without consulting you.

Examples:

- Gives dodgy characters access to your kids. You might suspect nothing because the adult doesn't seem dangerous on his or her own part. Someone who is not physically or psychologically capable of being a serious threat can still turn your child over to someone else who is, out of either poor judgment or actual bad intentions.
- Exposes your offspring to vices like drugs or pornography. Not necessarily as a pusher, or to bait them for sexual predation (though those are risks too), but often just as a bad influence. Once kids are habituated to vice, it doesn't seem like a big deal.
- Takes your daughter (or son) to have her ears pierced, without your knowledge or consent.
- Takes your daughter to get an abortion. The offender is commonly a feminist teacher or counselor. In many jurisdictions, this is a protected action and is effectively

encouraged. Teen Vogue magazine had an article about how to get an abortion without parents' knowledge or consent. Risks are not disclosed.
- Defames one of your kids. If it's really bad, it could lead to suicide.
- Encourages one of your kids to commit suicide. Usually this is another young person, but there have been a few cases of adults bullying and goading children into suicide.
- Installs a gender dysphoria in a young child; this phenomenon has turned into a pandemic. They punish children for gendered behavior, and reward them for being genderless, trans-gendered, or one of the new "synthetic genders" such as "polygender" or "xenogender". The culprit is usually a woman, often the mother but commonly enough it's someone with access to other people's children; judging from videos circulating on social media, it's rampant among teachers.
- Manipulates your teenager into questioning her gender, then put pressure on her to undergo a sex-change. There is currently a craze called "sudden-onset gender dysphoria," typically preceded by intense social pressure. At least one motive is to create trans-men to satisfy demand for a sexual fetish among both men and women for someone who looks superficially male, but retains female sex organs.
- Encourages your daughter to experiment first with herself, then on other girls. Encourages her to cruise bathrooms looking for them. This phenomenon is now

rampant. The purpose is to train girls to pursue recreational sex with other girls so they won't be interested in boys. One girl I am aware of ended up getting raped cruising the bathrooms in a park late at night, *after being encouraged to pursue this activity by a youth group leader.*
- An anti-natalist convinces your daughter that it's her duty to save the planet by never having children. This is most likely to happen without any explicit conversation; your daughter will pick it up unconsciously and mimetically from someone in a position of influence who has a negative attitude towards children or parenthood, or who encourages a lifestyle incompatible with having children.
- Shows children sex-toys, and possibly even demonstrates how to use them. When the targets are pre-pubescent children, the culprit is usually a man. When teenage girls, usually an adult woman. In both cases, the perpetrators will claim to be "mentoring" children (rather than admit to "grooming" them); be prepared to fight the sponsoring institution when you try to stop this activity or alert other parents to it.
- Recruits a teenager into a radical activist group whose activities include riots, threats, and harassment. This has become common; teachers and youth-group leaders are the typical culprits instigating this.

I got most of this list from personal observations of events close at hand. If you are naive about all of this, or worse, in denial ("we don't have that here"), it's time to stop being naive and stop being complacent.

Don't be overly-trusting of people in seeming leadership positions. You're a grown man; don't allow yourself to be cowed by imposed authority. There are predators among the ranks of teachers, counselors, coaches, clergy, and youth group leaders. Most of them are innocent; you can be wary and protective without the risk of dealing out false accusations or starting a "moral panic." You can pull your kids away from the influence of someone you don't trust without violating anyone's rights. Where young people without experience in life are concerned, trust has to be earned upfront. Proactively, systematically vet anyone with access to your children, then plan for ongoing monitoring. Every time there is a change of personnel, vet the new person and maintain as much of a watchful eye as possible. Don't be afraid to ask questions, and don't be afraid to say "NO!"

If someone with access to your child doesn't like you, or tries to isolate your child from you, that's a red flag for hostile intent. It's also a potential opportunity to turn your child against you, by doling out criticism of you, and handing out rewards when your child agrees, or withholding approval if they don't. Beware, this is more common than you probably realize, and dads are favorite targets because we're the ones they want to get out of their way, but also the ones more likely to be busy at work and not on hand to defend our own

> interests.
>
> If people with access to your children aren't 100% on-board with your values and goals, take your business elsewhere. As I type these words, western culture is breaking down dramatically, and there are a lot of creepy, cult-like behaviors going on in institutions parents are entrusting their kids to.

The new, non-negotiable rules for an untrustworthy society:

- Trust is not the default; trust has to be earned. Don't just assume your kids are safe with strangers unless you discover abuse later; you need to take proactive steps to prevent abuse before it happens. As hard as it is to prevent abuse, it's still easier than trying to mitigate the damage!
- Screening up front, followed by ongoing monitoring for any signs of trouble.
- Attempts to isolate your child from you, including scheduling frequent, non-family-oriented, remote activities, is a red flag.
- Hostility towards you is an instant deal-breaker. The very fact that dads deter trouble gives troublemakers a reason to be hostile towards us. It's also an opportunity for the bad actor to turn your child against you, which is more common than most dads probably realize.
- Have frank discussions with your kids regarding behaviors they must not tolerate and need to report to you. This may seem awkward or taboo, but it's better than trying to deal

with the aftermath of sexual abuse.
- Tell your kids up-front that adults telling them to keep secrets is a red flag for bad intentions, and remind them frequently to "tell us if they tell you not to tell us."
- You are responsible for not starting or contributing to false accusations. Individual lives, families, and even entire communities have been destroyed over false accusations motivated by reasons like wanting attention or covering up an indiscretion.

How to screen adults for access to children? Background checks are rendered useless when cover-ups and intimidation tactics by organized networks of activists and allies are the norm; it's not unusual that abusers have clean records, even after being caught multiple times. The ideal screening strategy would be a combination of background check, references, and interview, with all of these measures being disclosed in writing and agreed-to up-front by the prospective candidate by signature, with a lawyer overseeing the paperwork to reduce the risk of being sued.

In some contexts, the process is regulated by state agencies, but corruption and incompetence are the rule not the exception.

Headline news:
> *Berlin authorities placed children with pedophiles*
> by Rina Goldenberg, Deutsche Welle
> June 15, 2020

The 'Kentler Project' in West Berlin routinely placed homeless children with pedophile men, assuming they'd make ideal foster parents. A study has found the practice went on for decades.

Similar "projects" and "experiments" keep happening all over the world, usually with less publicity after a thorough cover-up.

Here's another type to watch out for: adults who influence children to make drastic, life-changing choices, for example, teachers who take it upon themselves to diagnose children as "trans", assign them new names and pronouns, and induce gender confusion that wasn't there before the teacher got hold of them. The institutions and the state are currently *protecting* adults who do this.

Bottom line: it is extremely unwise to go along with outsourcing responsibility for your children's safety and security—it's up to you, and you'll need to be willing to put up a fight.

Dads deter trouble

Kids tend to be safest with their dads around. Unfortunately, not always, but much more often than not.

> *"Family structure reflects the number of parents in the household and their relationship to the child; living arrangement reflects their marital or cohabitation status. Considering both factors, the NIS–4 classified children into six categories: living with two married biological parents, living with other married parents*

(e.g., step-parent, adoptive parent), living with two unmarried parents, living with one parent who had an unmarried partner in the household, living with one parent who had no partner in the household, and living with no parent. The groups differed in rates of every maltreatment category and across both definitional standards. Children living with their married biological parents [me: in practice, this usually means with their biological father present] universally had the lowest rate [me: of mistreatment in all mistreatment categories]."
Fourth National Incidence Study
of Child Abuse and Neglect (NIS–4)
Report to Congress
Executive Summary

Unfortunately, these types of government-funded studies are designed to frame the situation in ways that will not cause offense to politically-powerful groups, and in ways that don't argue against more government programs. The study I referenced above breaks the situation down in terms of various living arrangements, which might provide some useful information, but pointedly avoided breaking it down by what is by far the most significant factor of all: whether or not the children live with their biological father.

Dads deter trouble.

How did the influential political conservative I mentioned in the Introduction miss this factor? Well, for one thing, he wasn't looking for it.

How about the feminist I referred to in the Introduction? Let's zoom in on something she wrote that's a red-flag:

> *I contrast the individualized desire for my-child (to inherit my-property, my-name, my-physical-and-psychological characteristics) with the tendency of lesbian and "single" mothers to form extended families and with the belief that I hold that women-move naturally into more communal and cooperative settings than do men.*
> — Sally Miller Gearhart, *The future—if there is one—is female*

Redefinition alert: when feminists refer to "extended family", they're not referring to the way that people in patriarchal agrarian civilizations tend to live with their aunts, uncles, cousins, and grandparents all under one roof; they're referring to substitutes for family. They're referring to unrelated third-parties who drift in and out of the lives of women and children who depend on them. What's in it for whoever is supplying money or room and board? It's naive and unreasonable to expect something for nothing. Are they getting whatever they're after from over-the-hill mom, or from her sweet-sixteen daughter?

Non-consanguineous communal living arrangements, whether in cults or communes, have consistently proved themselves to be dangerous places for kids.

I've found numerous references to children being safest growing up with a dad at home, but haven't been able to discover any definitive third-party research regarding what specific thing dads do that prevents violence to kids. Rarely is it ever actually having to fight off aggressors and predators.

Here's one clue:

> "Children were somewhat more likely to be maltreated by female perpetrators than by males: 68% of the maltreated children were maltreated by a female, whereas 48% were maltreated by a male."
> —Fourth National Incidence Study of Child Abuse and Neglect (NIS–4)
> Report to Congress
> Executive Summary

68% + 48% = 116%; it goes over 100% because there's overlap where both a male and a female are abusing the kids. Bearing in mind that "a male" is statistically less likely to be the dad than some other man, whereas "a female" is usually the mother, but sometimes a grandmother or an aunt. So the most likely reasons children are safest living with you are

- You're less likely to abuse one of your own children than other potential caregivers.
- You're much less likely to assault or sexually abuse one of your own children than an unrelated man is.
- Your very presence is a deterrent to abuse by others.

You don't even need to do anything except exist close to your own kids to keep them relatively safer than otherwise!

The exceptional cases of paternal abuse are why I include so much advice about managing your own beliefs and emotions, and de-escalating situations before you lose your temper.

What if YOU are the stepdad or the adopted dad? I'm on your side too. Learning the skills in this book will help you engage your kids and bond with them. Cultivate protective, compassionate, paternal feelings for your kids. Know yourself well enough that inappropriate feelings don't catch you by surprise. Something that I've noticed among men who have good relationships with their step-kids is that they don't speak of "my wife's kids"; they consider any kid living under their roofs to be their responsibility and under their protection. I've also met several men who express a great deal of filial love and gratitude for their protective, paternal step-dad or adopted dad.

Learn how to calm distraught babies

This might seem like mom's job, but there are compelling reasons for you to know. An infant crying for hours on end can rattle most people's nerves to the breaking point. As likely the strongest member of the family, you would do well to know how to calm a distraught baby to prevent yourself, or for that matter, anyone else, from snapping.

The way NOT to deal with a crying baby is to shake it. With their big heads and fragile spines, it can kill or permanently damage them. Aside from knowing that yourself, warn other family members.

These things are all soothing to babies:

- Being held or wrapped ("swaddled") in a bundle (make sure they can breath freely!). It seems to be a reflex and probably

has something to do with reminding them of life in the womb.
- Rhythmic motion
- White noise (shushing sounds from yourself, or white noise from a machine)

Robert C. Hamilton, MD, a pediatrician in Santa Monica CA, has a video you can look for on video-hosting websites showing you his technique: How To Calm A Crying Baby - Dr. Robert Hamilton Demonstrates "The Hold" (Official)

Dads rescue kids

While your presence alone is enough to keep kids safe from some types of danger, there are other dangers that require action on your part. Dads rescue kids, sometimes at the cost of their own lives.

Zack Small, "the family alpha," has a story on his website about the time his young son slipped into the water and had to be rescued before he drowned.

I had an emergency once when one of my baby daughters picked a Passionflower leaf and immediately stuffed it down her throat whole, completely blocking her airway. Just like that, she was unable to breathe. I happened to be a few blocks from a hospital, and considered running for it (all that time, she wouldn't have been able to breathe), but then I cleared my mind, reached down her throat with my fingers, and pulled out the leaf. She resumed breathing straight-away as if nothing serious had happened. Handling emergencies is largely a matter of staying alert, keeping a clear mind, knowing how to handle common types of emergencies, and staying fit so that you can handle any physical challenges the emergency may entail.

It's also worth committing some time and resources to martial arts training, and specifically, something that will teach you to put up a credible defense. Many martial arts programs are more geared towards "movement" for yuppies who work as desk-jockeys; those won't help.

Teach your kids about the dark side of life

It's all well and good to protect your kids from danger. It's a strong instinct, one I am very conscious of myself, hence I was quick to bring it up.

But someday, I won't be there for my kids. They'll have situations they'll have to deal with when I'm not around. The older they get, the more that will happen. And soon enough, I'll be dead.

You might think that they'll pick up all the right thought patterns and values from you just by being around you, but I've discovered from personal experience that's not enough. Your kids are getting a lot of bad messages from influences other than you. You need to step up your game to counter-act them. After protecting kids from danger, teaching them to recognize and protect themselves from danger is the next most important thing dads do.

A bad message kids commonly get is that the Kosmos is conspiring to do them favors. Something we might call "pronoid" (opposite of paranoid) fantasies. They're all over children's literature and in entertainment for children.

Let me give you an example: years ago, I went looking through some packs in the local children's library consisting of books collected on a specific theme. I found one that was supposed to be about "farming", and checked it out for my daughter. Not ONE book in the pack had ANYTHING to do with real farming. Every single book was horrible, but the one that stood out in my mind was about a family whose chickens conspire to do them favors. They do homework, and clean up messes left by the children! What a way to teach responsibility to children!

Even worse is an entire genre of children's literature involving children being befriended by a "misunderstood" and persecuted monster of some sort. The most common variant is that the monster represents a seditious influencer (think communist). In other cases, the monster is a metaphor for a sexual predator.

Less sinister, but still harmful, are any number of overly rosy depictions of life:

- The city is full of "community helpers" who do their jobs out of a desire to serve you. In reality, at the very least, they want to get paid, and some of them are corrupt.
- The government exists to take care of you. In reality, governments regularly kill people, both overtly through war, and covertly through assassinations or as side-effects of

policy (eg triggering a famine or an epidemic).
- When a bully hurts you, and you turn around and be nice to the bully, the bully will be nice to you. This is a formula for getting kids (later, adults) trapped in abusive relationships where they unintentionally encourage more abusive behavior by rewarding it.
- The lion wants to be your friend. It's just a big, cuddly kitty. In reality, the lion wants to eat you.
- The big herbivore is a "gentle giant". In reality, they tend to be territorial. A hippopotamus will snap your body in half if it catches you in its pond.
- Let's not forget a new bizarre and dangerous trend: gender dysphorias are fun and totally healthy!

While reading to my kids, I routinely stop and correct unrealistic pronoid scenarios. "Cats don't really befriend mice, do they? That's right, they eat them!"

There's been a longstanding trend in children's literature and entertainment to avoid "scary" topics. A good example would be the longstanding opinion that the movie Bambi is "too traumatic" for children because Bambi's mother was shot dead.

What traumatizes children is NOT the knowledge that there are dangers in life. What traumatizes them is when their parents react to danger in a disempowering way. If a parent warns a child about a danger—say there were a rabies epidemic going around—and the parent is trembling with fear and using lots of over-the-top scary language, and the child is picking up on the parent's fear and becoming afraid themselves, THAT is how you later get a great hulk of a man who will run and scream if a squirrel pops out from behind a tree, because now he has a phobia. More generally, you can get all sorts of unhelpful reactions to problems if you don't nip those in the bud.

When you talk about danger, here is the way to do it:

- Keep it age-appropriate. But don't forget to bring it up when the right age comes around!
- Stay calm, rational, and matter-of-fact.
- Pay attention to the reaction of the child, and respond appropriately.
- Don't leave the child in a "problem state". Don't just talk about problems; move the conversation along to what we do to protect ourselves. Talk them through from the problem to the solution.

Here is a short list of broad topics to talk about:

- Hazards of the physical world
- Violence and crime
- Sexual predation
- Fraud (particularly the kind you get lured into with promises of unearned benefits)
- Deception

Protect your kids from the hazards of modern lifestyles

Healthy lifestyles probably started out as a mom-issue more than a dad-issue, because women do most of the shopping, seem to have more body-awareness than men do (they have to because of the complexity of their reproductive systems), and because nurturing was traditionally more of a maternal role than a paternal role. Things have changed dramatically in recent generations: the stakes have never been higher, and opinions regarding what constitutes a healthy lifestyle have never been as polarized. As a result, dads have not only gotten pulled into the fray, but are now also taking sides and getting as polarized as the moms. For that matter, you're more likely to do the hardware work needed to mitigate some of the hazards.

Civilized, and especially high-tech, lifestyles have created some new hazards to physical and mental health, including:

- Our bodies are still designed for hunter-gatherer diets, which are very different from civilized diets.
- There are a lot of pollutants recently introduced into the environment, that have never existed on the earth before humans manufactured them.
- Humans have always co-existed with bacteria. Any of them are harmful to us if they're in sufficient numbers and where they don't belong, but some are critical symbiants. Recently, we've lost access to some of our symbiant bacteria, both by no longer being exposed to their habitats (e.g. loss of access- to soil bacteria), and by killing them off indiscriminately with antibiotics or other drugs.
- Our ancestors spent a lot of their time outdoors, where sunshine striking our skin powered the process that creates vitamin D. Indoor living starves us for vitamin D.

- In a natural environment, it's bright and sunny in the daytime, and dark at night. Our eyes have sensors monitoring the amount of blue light we're being exposed to, to synchronize our bodily functions to the cycles of day and night. Artificial lighting throws off those cycles.

I often hear rebuttals that we live longer than our ancestors did. Generally true, but that only means we've traded set of problems for another. Maladaptation to modern living is worse than is generally realized. The mainstream media touches on the consequences only marginally, and solutions are usually framed only in terms of collective action. You're better off taking action yourself; collective solutions are slow and often ham-fisted.

The problem is cumulative, because some of the pollutants are extremely persistent in the environment, some of the bad habits are getting more and more entrenched, and because the impact is getting into our "epigenetics", meaning that genes are getting switched on or off the wrong way, persistently from generation to generation.

Sometimes it's hard to know exactly what measures to take. Too much information, most of it irrelevant and distracting, is as bad as too little. Much of it is misinformation (wrong information propagated by people who don't know better) or disinformation (intentional deceptions). While trying to learn about endocrine disruptors in plastics, I found diametrically-contradictory information. Even experts can get things wrong because expertise tends to be highly-specialized these days, but the hazards have to be analyzed in terms of multiple sciences like biology, chemistry, and statistics.

The good news is that the risks tend to be asymmetric: there's no harm in NOT eating sucralose. It's inconvenient, but there's no harm in avoiding *all* plastics for storing food and water.

The problem is so big I can't do it justice here; when I tried, I found the amount of information I was trying to convey would have swamped the rest of the book. Until I clear up my queue for another book, here are some very high-level tips to promote your family's physical and mental health:

- Minimize fast-food and convenience foods.
- For cooking or for eating raw in salads, choose a stable oil that doesn't have an excess of omega-6 fats compared to omega-3. The ideal ratio is probably around 1:1, but diets in western countries are typically around 16:1. You need both, but super-abundant omega-6 crowds out scarcer omega-3. Some of the worst offenders are commodity seed-oils like corn oil, sunflower oil, and soy oil. Generic "vegetable oil" is a bad choice.
- We avoid deep-fried foods, or for that matter, foods stir-fried with really hot oil. If you want fried food as an occasional treat (not daily fare), try air-frying using a modest amount of a stable oil rich in monounsaturates, like olive oil. Whatever you do, don't deep-fry food and then keep re-using the damaged oil.
- We serve non-starchy, fibrous, colorful vegetables daily. The Brassicas such as broccoli, cabbage or collards, Brussels

sprouts, kale, mustard greens, and bok choi are particularly good choices for many reasons, including their content of fiber, folacin, glucosinolates, and antioxidants.
- We supplement vitamins D and K regularly. You can find dedicated supplements that contain D3 and the elusive menaquinone-7 form of K2, which your ancestors got from exposure to soil bacteria and from eating ruminants who were grazing on natural grassland. NB: if you take blood thinners, ask your doctor before supplementing K2.
- Talk to your expectant wife about supplementing vitamins D and B9 (folacin) during pregnancy. A good-quality pre-natal supplement should contain both of these, but check the amounts, because the supplement might be her only significant source of the vitamin D.
- Avoid plastic water bottles generally. Some soft plastic water-bottles have labels assuring you that the product contains "No Bisphenol A". What they fail to disclose is that they probably contain phthalate! Rigid plastics like polycarbonate have labels reassuring you they contain no phthalates. Instead, they're the ones that contain Bisphenol A.
- Avoid food cans lined with Bisphenol A. As of this writing, about 10% of them still are.
- Beware of plastic (PVC or PEX) pipes. They might leach chemicals into your drinking water, they are reportedly permiable to some chemicals such as gasoline, and they are vulnerable to breaking down in high heat, which could contaminate water flowing through them.
- Avoid using plastic containers (including bags) for storing food, and especially avoid putting hot food in them, or using

them to heat foods in the microwave. Just avoid them altogether as much as possible. Use containers made from glass, wood, natural fiber produce bags, wax-infused natural fibers (instead of plastic cling-wrap), or even the highly synthetic but relatively non-reactive substance silicone. I suggest avoiding silicone for cooking, though, because it does react if the temperature is high enough.

- Avoid cookware treated with non-stick chemicals. Personally, I like cast iron, which is naturally somewhat non-stick, not to mention durable. I have a waffle iron & some bakeware that are coated with ceramic instead of with PTFEs. Most of the rest of my cookware is stainless steel; stuff sticks to it, but at least it's durable and fairly non-reactive. There is now bakeware coated with silicone instead of PTFE; be careful not to overheat it.

- Give preference to natural fibers over synthetic fibers for clothing, carpeting, and furnishings. Easier said than done, because synthetics are now the norm, but see what you can find. The reason it matters is because fibers tend to get worn down into dust, and the synthetic chemicals can end up in your body from breathing them in or ingesting them.

- Avoid scented, lotion-like toiletries in plastic containers as much as possible (especially while your wife is pregnant!). Consider using unscented bar soap for washing hands and body, and unscented bar shampoo for washing your hair, both packaged in paper wrappers.

- Daily time outdoors for the whole family, in as natural an environment as you can find close to where you live. If you have a safe, fenced back-yard, send the kids out to play in it

daily. If you don't have one, regular trips to local parks.
- Get into the habit of listening to your body. Are you hungry? Sleepy? Feeling sick? Depressed? Pay attention and encourage your family members to do the same.
- Install a utility on all your computer screens, cell phones, and mobile computing devices that shifts the screen to a yellowish-brownish or reddish cast in evenings, to reduce the blue light you're exposed to after sunset. Make sure the utility is set to operate automatically.
- Budget your time with electronic devices; don't allow yourself or your family members to get addicted to electronics. Especially watch out for addictions to pornography, gaming, & toxic social media. Displace excessive time spent with electronics with time spent on family activities, both recreational and family projects. At our house, Friday is family game night, and Sunday is electronics detox day.
- Install dimmer switches in your house wherever you tend to occupy in the evening hours, and turn down the lights in the evening. LED Light bulbs that turn yellower as they're dimmed (make sure the bulbs are, indeed, dimmable!) are a plus, though unfortunately the ones I've found myself are still very yellow at full output.
- Discourage frequent or late-night snacking.
- Regular "face-time" with family and friends, for every member of the family. Notice when teens and young adults are isolating themselves. Organize your own regular family-oriented activities, such as family suppers and game-nights. This is more important than the so-called "socialization"

supposedly associated with school-time. Important update for lockdowns: if you're not allowed to visit family and friends in person, connect any way you can, by email, texting or internet chats, phone calls, and even old-fashioned letters. Set up reminders to make contact at least several times a week. Do not allow yourself, your family members, or your friends to feel lonely and socially-isolated.

The problem of maintaining healthy intestinal flora would need a book all by itself, and indeed there are already several on the market; here's a title I've read myself:

The Microbiome Solution: A Radical New Way to Heal Your Body from the Inside Out
by Dr. Robynne Chutkan M.D.
Avery Publishing

There's an audiobook version available on Audible.com.

One thing worth mention in passing: you're probably not eating enough organically-grown raw vegetables. Aside from eating more of them, something else that might help is to ferment those organic vegetables in their own natural microbes, and eat those (eg home-made Sauerkraut or naturally-fermented kimchee).

Here's some additional reading about the hazards associated with endocrine disruptors:

Count Down: How Our Modern World Is Threatening Sperm Counts, Altering Male and Female Reproductive Development,

and Imperiling the Future of the Human Race.
By Shanna Swann, with Stacey Colino
Simon and Schuster

There's an audio version available on Audible.com.

And here's a book linking circadian rhythms with body functions and health:

The Circadian Code: Lose Weight, Supercharge Your Energy, and Transform Your Health from Morning to Midnight
by Satchin Panda PhD
Rodale Books

There's an audio version available on Audible.com.

Appendix I
Beliefs that cause trouble

Children are born bad. They have "original sin."

This is a gross misinterpretation of the concept of original sin. Original sin has more to do with being born into a world of suffering and alienation; you don't make it any better by having negative attitudes towards children. Children are born perfect. They just haven't been trained how to behave yet.

Boys are bad.

Male and female mammals differ by a single chromosome that only has a few genes on it. All they do is trigger a hormonal chain-reaction that turns sex-linked genes up or down. Mostly we're about the same: women and girls have two eyes, two ears, a nose, and a mouth, and so do men and boys. Men and boys even have nipples!

The differences that do exist are all quantitative, not qualitative. Women are courageous and men are nurturing; it's only a matter of degree.

The differences that cause trouble have to do with risk profiles; males are more prone to risky behaviors than females are. It's because we're more expendable in the greater scheme of things because sperm are more abundant than eggs. That doesn't mean that men are immoral. It does mean that most bank robbers are men...but by the same token, so are most heroes running into burning buildings to rescue trapped children.

The same principles apply to the differences between boys and girls.

When parents have trouble with their boys, it's because the parents don't know how to relate to them and engage them. It's particularly pathetic that this is true even of many dads who don't know how to relate to sons despite having been boys themselves once. The problem has gotten worse in recent generations due to misandric influences.

You need to put the fear of God into them so that they won't do it again

It's unwise to train children to react emotionally to problems above and beyond regret for the costs of their mistakes. Strong emotions displace rational problem-solving capacities. It's also not a good idea to direct their attention to themselves and how they feel. Instead you want them to react rationally, and you want to direct their attention to the feelings and rights of other people.

Children misbehave more than they used to because their parents don't spank them any more.

It is naive to assume that if parents say that they don't believe in hitting children, then indeed they don't even when no other adults are around to witness it. Research involving nanny-cams and audio recording devices indicates otherwise. This public virtue, private vice situation can warp your sense of reality if you buy into the false self-assessment and then judge the results of bad parenting. Parents don't usually hit their kids cold-bloodedly; it's usually after losing control of a situation and then losing their tempers. Gentleness with children is not a self-image or a political ideology; it's a matter of training to respond appropriately to misbehavior, and also of emotional self-discipline.

Misbehavior isn't caused by lack of beatings; it's caused by lack of training. The lack of training is because children are not around their parents as much as they used to be, and because most parents have at best only a vague sense of how to train their children to behave in the first place.

Getting a spanking is better than getting hit by a car.

True but irrelevant. If a child wanders into the street and gets hit by a car, it wasn't for lack of a spanking; it was for lack of training not to go into the street, and for lack of supervision until the training took hold. Abuse and neglect go hand-in-hand more often than not.

If you hit a child for misbehavior, they won't do it again, but if they do, that means you were too lenient the first time and have to punish them more severely. The more they misbehave, the more severely you have to punish them.

"Insanity is doing the same thing over and over again and expecting a different result."—Narcotics Anonymous

Violence and threats of violence are not very effective as deterrents to mischief, because most misbehavior isn't consciously planned. The right way to prevent bad habits is to interrupt them and give feedback in the form of a warning, a reprimand, or non-violent consequences.

If you tell a child not to do something, they can make a choice right then and there not to do it again.

Patterns of behavior, including your own, are overwhelmingly unconscious. A child can not consciously override their unconscious habits. You, the parent, need to interrupt bad habits and give feedback.

If you ignore misbehavior, hopefully it will go away.

If you ignore misbehavior, it will continue until you lose your temper. Losing your temper will only make the situation worse by teaching children to respond to problems emotionally instead of rationally.

If you ask a child nicely to do something or stop doing something, they'll feel obliged to comply in order to be polite.

You will not be the person to teach your child via social pressure; that will be their peers. By the time they're teenagers, it will finally dawn on you that they care more about offending their friends than they do about offending you. By the way, the more you nag them, the faster they'll learn to ignore it as noise (more likely, they'll learn to ignore their mothers; either way, nagging backfires). Be politely firm with your children, and back it up with the "three strikes" method.

If you tell children that their behavior is bothering you, they'll stop it.

Accept that other people have their own motives that do not revolve around your needs. Work with those motives instead of against them.

Appendix I: Beliefs that cause trouble

If you tell a child "stop that!", they'll stop what they are doing. If not, yell louder, because that will help.

Nature abhors a vacuum. Do you really expect them to suddenly go inert and do nothing? Instead of saying "stop that!," start counting them using the "three strikes and you're out" method. Then fill the vacuum by finding a better use for their time.

If you tell children to do something, or not do something, enough times, then they'll comply. If what you're doing isn't working, do it more until it starts working.

If what you're doing isn't working, try something else. The methods described here will work quickly most of the time, except in cases of deeply-entrenched habits that got that way because they were let go too long. There is also the possibility that you have an existing belief or habit of your own that's so entrenched, you're oblivious to the way it interferes with your ability to objectively assess the situation. In that case you could try swallowing your pride and asking someone you consider a good father if he notices anything that you don't.

Children have to be allowed to do whatever they want, or they'll be developmentally stunted.

Children are goal-seeking and learn from feedback. Giving them feedback, in a respectful and compassionate way, helps them learn.

A time-out or reprimand will emotionally scar a child for life.

It's not calm feedback that emotionally scars children. It's a parent's rage that terrorizes them, or shame and ridicule that train them to respond to problems with self-loathing. If you stay calm, non-violent, and respectful, there's no emotional trauma to trigger a self-esteem problem. Assign non-violent consequences in a calm, rational, respectful manner.

By the way, people who claim that they don't believe in timeouts or reprimands do hand out punishments and rewards all the time; they simply don't recognize them as such. If you're going to give feedback, better do it consciously and do it right.

My kids will hate me if I discipline them or tell them "no". Better leave that to mom.

A self-defeating prophesy, the kind that happens precisely because of the misguided measures taken to try to prevent it from happening. Nobody likes a wimp. The kids unconsciously infer that you're mostly superfluous in the grand scheme of things and mom is the only real parent (you on the other hand get relegated to "problem child" status). Never telling them "no" doesn't make them like you; it turns them into spoiled brats whose increasingly unrealistic expectations of life will eventually cause them to turn on you. Taking charge in a calm, rational, respectful way fosters respect and a sense of security ("it'll be OK; dad's here to set things right"), and that will *improve* your relationship with them.

Appendix I: Beliefs that cause trouble

Television didn't hurt me growing up.

Don't flatter yourself. Most people have become so habituated to what is on television that it doesn't occur to them that anything might be wrong with either the programming itself, or the whole paradigm of sitting in front of a "lobotomy box." Aside from the programming itself, watching television is "passive attention." It starves out "active attention." Lack of capacity for much active attention is popularly known as "attention deficit." The cure is turning off the television, computer, and cell phones, and going outside to play.

I'm a good father.

You can't be anything. You can only do. Self-images distort perceptions. Don't be like Joan Crawford. She was an actress who cultivated the image of a kind, high-minded woman, but behind closed doors, she was viciously cruel to her adopted children. Believing that they are "good parents" is how some parents are oblivious to their own parenting mistakes. Pay attention to what you're doing, not what you think you are.

Listen to the experts. Raise your kids the way they tell you.

You are responsible for raising your own kids according to your own informed good judgment. You might lack experience, or an understanding of the consequences of your choices, which is why you need to seek out the best information and advice that is available to you, and then you have to evaluate it yourself before acting on it. Ultimately, what you contribute to raising your own kids are the consequences of your own conscious choices; don't fail to make them by just going the path of least resistance.

What about me? First of all, nobody's propping me up as an expert; I'm just one dad sharing hard-won insights and experience with another dad...and encouraging you to make your own conscious, informed decisions.

Pandora Hightower does NOT approve of your child-rearing methods, and she's a world-class expert!

You're damn right she doesn't, and she's sicced her hordes of minions on me too. In all seriousness, Pandora Hightower is a fictional stereotype of a certain type of parenting "expert" who believes that children spontaneously "develop" according to age norms, instead of according to the feedback they get. There's also another popular parenting fad that came out of feminist circles that I parodied as "affirmative parenting." It has to do with affirming certain conceits that some parents want to believe about themselves and their children, and has no scientific backing that I'm aware of. It's an easy sale to make. I'd rather tell you what you need to know to get good results. Fair enough?

Appendix II
Patterns that cause trouble

Watch out for these parenting patterns:

Problem: Parent says "no," "stop it," makes a threat, or criticizes what the child did, but never interrupts the behavior or assigns consequences until the situation escalates to violence. This is Barbara's problem.
Solution: Implement "three strikes and you're out".

Problem: Parent's mood is largely a function of the child's behavior. The parent emotionally overreacts to the child's behavior, often becoming enraged when the child does not behave as expected. The child may react with fear or anger, neither of which address the problem. Aside from escalating misbehavior, the child tends to pick up the parents habit of emotional over-reaction.
Solution: Increase emotional self-control and accept that the child is not responsible for maintaining the your mood; you are.

Problem: Parent is too self-absorbed to notice the child's behavior until and unless the child acts up. The result is more misbehavior. The child is being rewarded by not only getting whatever the goal of the misbehavior was, but also, if it escalates enough, with (negative) attention from the otherwise self-absorbed parent.

Solution: Give the child enough attention that you notice violations of safety rules and other people's rights, and also be mindful of the child's own physical and emotional needs. Some undivided attention should be regularly scheduled exclusively for the child. That would include having friendly conversations with your child, playing with your child, or engaging your child in shared activities. Start re-examining your priorities and values if this seems like a burden rather than a joy.

Problem: Parent expresses desires instead of clear instructions, or vague suggestions instead of clear, firm rules, and then hopes that the child will take the hint. Parent asks for permission or consent instead of giving direct orders for non-negotiable issues, such as "would you like to stop swinging that stick at other people?" or "Can I hold your hand while we cross the busy street?" Overall parenting behavior is "wimpy" and "wishy-washy". These behaviors tend to occur among parents who are too dependent and needy for approval. They tend to result in tyrannical behaviors in the children. Ironically, children don't even particularly want to be in charge; it leaves them feeling insecure.

This is starting to turn into an epidemic among fathers, who are increasingly rewarded for emasculated behaviors and punished for taking charge. Often they feel insecure about their place in the family and are treated as obsolete. Their own accommodating behavior actually reinforces the pattern by validating the wrong expectations.

Solution: Take responsibility and take charge. The child can not be left in charge of the household, the family, or his or her own personal safety.

Leadership is not about bullying others to get your own way; leadership is about sharing experience and insights that benefit everyone. Ordering a subordinate at work to work overtime without getting credit for it, and ordering a frightened child to jump out of a burning building in order to escape certain death are both instances of giving orders...but with different outcomes. There's nothing wrong with taking charge as long as you do so for the benefit of everyone involved.

Problem: Parent tries to buy love, affection, and approval from the child. This is Doug's problem and it has long been common among fathers. The consequence is usually a strong sense of entitlement in the child, and often insecurity too as they get stuff instead of emotional support. The intent is to get love and respect, but it backfires.

Solution: To earn love and respect, there is no substitute for time and attention. Your offspring's attitude towards you is a function of the emotions they experienced while you were around. Being vaguely aware that you paid for their meals and perks does nothing to attach warm, loving, respectful emotions to their thoughts concerning you.

Problem: Dad surrenders responsibilities to day-care, schools, churches and youth groups, television, the internet, and to mom.

Solution: Beware that any institution that attracts families with children also attracts people who should not have access to them. Also beware that if you are superfluous, you will be treated accordingly.

Reclaim responsibility and leadership. That does mean fighting the current, because you are certain to arouse resistance and indignation from pushy people within your social circles, but the alternative leads to heartbreak.

Appendix III
Situations that cause trouble

Discipline breaks down at school or daycare
There are problems with discipline in schools and daycare beyond the scope of this document. I can't fix those problems and neither can you. You might never even recognize them, because they tend to hide behind pretexts that you might not realize are phony. Or you might not know about them at all, because you're busy at work while they're happening. The best you can do is to be alert for problems and be ready to take whatever steps are necessary to mitigate them.

Your first line of defense is to put off daycare as much and as long as possible. Ask yourself if there are ways you could arrange or re-arrange your lifestyle to use as little daycare as possible. Preferably, none.

Second, give your children the right expectations regarding treating others respectfully, and being treated respectfully in return.

Your next line of defense is to pro-actively talk to your children about what goes on at school or daycare. Be aware that young children may not have a strong sense of their own rights and responsibilities. Older children, especially around puberty, often turn secretive and extremely self-conscious. They may feel uncomfortable about talking about what happens at school. That's all the more reason you need to establish a deep rapport with your children so that they feel comfortable talking to you about personal matters.

You need to be willing to draw a line in the sand regarding what you will not tolerate at school or daycare. If that line is stepped over, you need to find a different arrangement.

Discipline breaks down whenever children are cared for by certain relatives

Bear in mind that free babysitting services come with strings attached.

In any case, don't leave your kids with anyone you have reason not to trust, and that includes people with diminished capacities, and people who show signs of poor emotional control or impulse control.

There might be situations that are not entirely within your control, for example, in a divorce situation where a court has assigned primary custodianship to your ex-wife. Do your best to compensate with your own influence, and don't be quick to give up.

There's a vast grey area of relatives who are not abusive, but lax in discipline, perhaps out of a desire to please their grandchildren or nieces and nephews, or perhaps just not knowing how to take charge of the situation.

Explain the "Three strikes and you're out" rule. It's simple enough that you might get some compliance. Don't count on it though, which is why you also need to explain to children that while the rules might be different at someone else's home, the rules you enforce in your own home will remain firmly in place.

Also, remind them up-front to be on their best behavior outside of your home.

Child is throwing a temper tantrum

You blew it. Once children are emotionally over-loaded, they've temporarily lost their ability to make a conscious choice regarding how they're going to respond to you or to the situation.

Don't respond with anger on your own part; it will only make the situation worse by limiting your own ability to respond rationally.

You can't talk or bully a child out of an emotional meltdown. Trying to do so and then getting frustrated is how enraged parents sometimes end up beating their kids to death. Instead, remove the child from public attention. If it's at home, escort the child to his or her room. If in public, escort (that probably means "carry") the child to an out-of-the-way spot, and arrange the situation to prevent harm to the child or others. Then let the emotion burn itself, out. Say as little as possible, and don't react.

Don't talk about what happened until the child is totally calm and back in control. Think about what happened, and make a plan for how to avoid the confrontation that triggered the tantrum in the first place. Solicit and obtain cooperation from the child. If the child says "no, I won't get mad again the next time we have brussels sprouts," then chances are, that will be the case, although you would do well not to push the envelop.

Keep in mind that children need to build up tolerance for whatever triggered the meltdown. For example, if a child became frustrated over a long wait or a long, uncomfortable ride, don't expect the child to handle it any better next time without building up to it. If a child can't wait an hour, don't try an hour next time; try a wait that's well within their tolerances.

Whatever you do, don't just repeat the situation that triggered the meltdown in the first place and expect a different result.

Child doesn't listen to you

Many parents have a habit of giving orders or criticism from afar, and then wondering why children don't listen. After a while, the parent's voice is just noise. If it's a serious matter, you need be willing to stop all distractions, get up close, get down on their level, a hand on the shoulder, draw the child in, lock eye contact, and build rapport.

The same misbehavior keeps happening, over and over, with no improvement

There are too many potential causes for this problem to zero in on any one without knowing the situation, but the important thing to understand is that it's being caused by something one or both parents are doing or not doing. It's not the child's fault; the child behaves as trained to behave. Assuming that you are promptly and consistently interrupting the misbehavior and giving feedback, first of all, make sure that rapport is solid. If the child is barely aware of your presence and isn't really listening to a word you're saying, there's your problem. Second, check for unintentional rewards for misbehavior; some common ones are getting the parent's attention, or manipulating the parent's mood. This is the hard part because you might be having difficulty seeing the unintended reward if your judgment is being clouded by a mistaken belief. You might try recruiting a 3rd party to witness the situation and give an assessment.

One more possibility is when a habit has become so entrenched due to earlier lack of correction, that it has become commensurately hard to break. In that case, interrupting it PROMPTLY and giving feedback should wear it down. It's important though that the behavior be interrupted before it completes. If it's something you only find out about after the fact, and then scold the child about some time later, the child first of all might not associate the scolding to the behavior, but instead will just learn to tune you out. There is an art to after-the-fact discipline, whereby you need to bring up what the child did, associate it to unpleasant consequences ("you're grounded for a week!"), and solicit a firm intention to comply next time.

Generally "rowdy," unfocused behavior. Child has difficulty finishing one activity before starting another. You find it hard to get and keep the child's attention.

The child needs to build up more ability to manage their attention, and more impulse control. Eliminate passive-attention activities like television, video games, and computer time until the problem is under control, then keep them under a strict budget. Preferably, the television budget is zero; it's really a very harmful medium.

Correspondingly increase active-attention activities. Spend some time each day making plans with your child. Play games that require following rules. Use objective "mediators" such as "you have to stay on the play-mat while you play this game," "remember to stay on your carpet square holding teddy-bear while we listen to the story," and "you have to stay here until the timer goes off." "Mediators" are props that help children remember rules. For example, if there's a rule that one child has to get off a slide before another one starts down, and the children are constantly ignoring the rule, you could have them pass around a token giving them the right to go down the slide. It seems strange that they can observe the rule better with the token than without it, but they respond to and are aware of external objects more than internal alarms.

Child doesn't do daily activities such as getting ready for school or bed in a timely or organized manner.
The most likely reason is lack of enough routine and structure. Most repetitive behaviors, good or bad, are habits. Good habits don't form unless there's enough of a pattern in a child's life. For example, if bed-time is determined when you just somewhat arbitrarily decide that it's getting late and it's time for bed, then your kids are not developing a good habit of getting ready for bed in a predictable manner. If there is a specific bed-time, it's easier to stick to it, and then easier to get up in the morning at the corresponding wake-up time.

Appendix III: Situations that cause trouble

Child refuses to finish an activity (such as playing) and move along to something else

Is there enough organization in your life that children know what to expect? Do you provide them with cues that signal that a transition is coming?

Did you give 5 minutes warning? Did you establish rapport, then solicit and receive firm confirmation that the child understands? Children will usually comply if they have the expectation that the activity is ending. They're even more likely to comply if you have asked for, and obtained, their agreement to end the activity within the specified number of remaining minutes.

A common, and needless, variation of this problem is when a parent tells a child who is engaged in a favored activity to come and do something else, without any warning, or without letting the child finish his current activity. Instead of saying "come and fold laundry," it works better to say "in 5 minutes, I'm going to call you to please come help me...". You don't like being abruptly interrupted either.

Child makes some sort of mind-numbing mess

For example, writes extensive marks over one or more walls in permanent ink. Paints the sofa. Scatters flour all over the carpeting and furniture in 3 different rooms. Colors his or her own body in indelible ink. Stains his or her best clothes. That sort of thing. Usually only happens with toddlers or just a little older, but sometimes involves older kids as the result of "science experiments."

Take it in good humor, though try not to laugh. Life is too precious to spoil it being uptight. If there has been a previous incident, assign consequences. Assign older children to clean up their own messes and make good on any damage done. In the case of younger children, an adult will need to organize the cleanup operation, but make sure that the perpetrator is involved. Emphasize that we take responsibility for our own actions.

One or both parents have difficulty managing the behavior of boys

Girls tend to pay more attention to people than boys do. Boys tend to reserve more of their attention to objects that might be useful. As a result, it's harder to establish rapport with boys than it is with girls.

This is not a problem in itself. The problem is parents who don't accept that he's not a girl and don't accommodate the differences.

Put a little more effort into establishing rapport. Get down on his level, put a hand on his shoulder, and make strong eye contact. Solicit and wait for an agreement on the resolution.

Another difference between the sexes that is not really a problem except to the extent that some parents make it so is that boys think in terms of rules rather than in terms of other people's feelings. A girl is more likely to think in terms of "she wouldn't like it if I hit her", whereas a boy is more likely to think in terms of "whoever hits first is at fault".

Appendix III: Situations that cause trouble

One situation in which this difference in perspectives goes wrong is when a mother gives a boy a rule, and then becomes angry when he conforms to the rule but not her intention. For example, a mother might punish him by telling him he can't go to a friend's house after school, and then she's surprised and irritated when the boy calls the friend over to his own house. Fathers are probably less prone to making this mistake because we also tend to think in terms of rules, not other people's intentions.

Boys are overall more aggressive than girls. This isn't a problem in itself either except to the extent that parents fail to set appropriate boundaries and channel it into appropriate activities such as sports. Good-natured rough-and-tumble behavior is not necessarily a problem until and unless it escalates to the point that it results in injuries or hurt feelings. Outright bullying is always a problem. Give feedback, teach him to be mindful of the rights and feelings of others, tell him what the rule is, and assign consequences appropriate for the offense.

Some misguided fathers think of bullying towards their sons as an opportunity for character-development rather than a possibly life-threatening hazard. They think he should be able to "handle himself" without assessing the specific risks of the situation or giving him any instruction on how to do so. What if the other boy is twice his size? Armed? What if it's a whole gang? What if he does defend himself—and gets gets arrested after an unsympathetic school administration calls the police on him?

If you want your sons to be able to defend themselves, then sign them up for martial arts training (serious training for self-defense, not "movement" for yuppies). In the meantime, take action if they're being bullied. If a boy is being bullied, and adults know about it but refuse to help him, how do you suppose he'll react? "They protect some kids, but not me, so they must not care about me. I must not be good enough." His self-esteem will plunge.

Here's a book to read together that showed up after I'd already raised all of my own sons, but comes highly recommended from several buddies of mine:

Way of the Warrior Kid: From Wimpy to Warrior the Navy SEAL Way: A Novel
by Jocko Willink and Jon Bozak
Di Angelo Publications

Young child shows aggression towards a parent

For example, a young child says "I hate you" or calls the mother a "bitch," or hits or kicks her. I don't pretend to know every possible reason this happens, but whenever I have observed it, it has consistently involved an emotionally-over-reactive parent, almost always the mother.

The parent's emotional over-reaction to whatever the child says or does turns into an unintentional reward (negative attention is preferable to none at all). The more upset she gets, the more it rewards the behavior. Often the emotions of the parent and child just keep feeding off each other.

This is a tricky one to solve because the parent will be tempted to disown responsibility for the problem. Don't be surprised if you get blamed for it; the assumption will be that it must be something you're doing, or not doing.

Once the blame-game is resolved, the solution is simple: stop reacting emotionally to what the child says or does. You can still assign consequences for hitting, kicking, calling bad names, and being otherwise abusive, but without emotional reactions or negative attention; in fact, it's best to withdraw attention after assigning consequences, especially attention from the over-reactive parent. For example, the father could put the child in the corner while the mother withdraws attention.

Among older children, assuming it's not an ongoing problem such as the previous one, it's a different story and it impacts dads even more often than moms; my best advice in this case would be to be alert for bad influences, and by bad influences, I mean one or more people badmouthing you and rewarding your child for agreeing and punishing them for disagreeing.

Argument among young children (yelling, screaming, but no hitting)

Physically separate the participants enough so that they disengage from each other and eventually calm down. If you can get their attention, talk them through what happened and how the argument could have been avoided. If you can't get them to engage you instead of each other, then give them both time-outs and talk about it later.

Fight among young children involving hitting, kicking, or other physical harm

Physically separate the combatants enough so that they disengage each other. If there is one clear aggressor, send the aggressor away for a time-out, then require the aggressor to apologize to the victim when the time-out is over. If the fight escalated evenly or it's hard to tell, don't punish both without first trying to find out what happened. If you can get their attention, talk them through what happened and how the fight could have been avoided. If not, give them both time-outs and talk about it later.

Child is distraught—perhaps crying hysterically or whimpering

I would have thought what to do is obvious, but I am adding this scenario after recently witnessing a mother totally ignore her extremely distraught son in a store. EDIT: I have since encountered a meme going around in feminist circles that helping a distraught child to calm down is "an act of violence"! Those are the exact words used, "an act of violence." They think children should be "free" to experience whatever emotions are seizing them up.

    Problems aren't resolved by ignoring them. Allowing a child to be traumatized with emotions he or she doesn't know how to process is not only cruel, but counter-productive since the child will now associate some thing, activity, or incident with emotional trauma. Then the parents are surprised when child becomes extremely uncooperative and agitated the next time the same or similar situation happens! Neither is this particular problem solved by smacking children, which is what abusive parents do. "Stop that crying, or I'll give you something to cry about!"

Instead, get down on the child's level, look the child in the face, soothe the child with a calm voice and calming gestures (for example, rubbing the child's shoulder or back in a comforting manner), and find out what is wrong. If you already know what's wrong, you can still ask how the child feels. Don't talk too much, though, and don't force the child to respond. You can respect a child's feelings without leaving him or her in a bad place.

Child expresses anger or rage—such as throwing something after asked to give it back, or calls someone else a bad name

Stay calm. Children do not learn emotional control from emotionally-over-reactive parents. If the outburst is unlikely to escalate, then calmly assign consequences for the outburst. If it is likely to escalate, wait it out and talk about it later. Suggest a retreat to a bedroom not as punishment, but as a refuge in which to calm down.

Child demands unearned treat or favor...such as buying a toy or some sweets

Don't buy anything on a child's impulsive whim. If the child badgers for it, issue "strikes" using the "3 strikes and you're out" method.

Child refuses to do something, such as a chore or practicing a lesson, OR, child doesn't refuse, but doesn't follow through either

Most parents get this wrong, because they're angered by the child's lack of obedience. You on the other hand can be the mature, responsible dad, stay calm and cool, and get it right. One common complication I have noticed is social pressure from teachers to punish children for not doing something. If a teacher is pressuring you to punish your child because she doesn't know how to motivate children, then calmly, diplomatically resist that pressure.

Generally, you don't punish a child for not doing an assigned task, aside from the possibility of natural consequences of what they have not done. You don't punish a child for not doing chores or homework—though privileges can and should be out of reach until assignments are completed, not as punishment, but as the way priorities are routinely structured to make rewards contingent on performance. The three obstacles that need to be overcome are lack of building up to the level of self-discipline to accomplish the task, lack of motivation, and lack of commitment from the child.

Start with expectations that are realistically within the child's willingness and ability to accomplish them. Then reward only the child's top-performance. That means you don't make awards for achievements once they become routine, but only now and then for mastering new responsibilities. To handle lack of commitment, you need first of all to motivate commitment, and second of all, you need to ask for it and obtain it.

> "Are you going to finish your homework before 9pm?"
> (evades eye contact) "Yeah...I guess."

That's as good as "No way!"; the child has no intention of trying. You need to get back a firm "yes" because anything less is a sign of resistance; the only reason the child isn't saying "no" is because he knows what is expected of him and is trying to placate you without actually making any real commitment.

> "Are you going to finish your homework before 9pm?"
> (evades eye contact) "Uh...yeah...I guess...".
> "Hmmm...that doesn't sound like a firm answer. Are you sure?"
> (looks you in the eye) "YES!"
> "Thanks. I appreciate your willingness to commit to having your homework done by 9."

What if, after giving you a firm commitment, your offspring still manages to completely fail to do something as agreed upon? That shouldn't happen very often, but when it does, don't criticize, and do take away privileges, because privileges have to be earned.

Child lies to you

Many parents over-react to this one. You really do want to nip it in the bud because you don't want your child to start a habit of lying, but you don't need to do anything violent or cruel.

Don't get angry, and if it's too late for that, take a deep breath, exhale slowly with a sigh, calm down, and then deal with the situation.

Don't call the child a liar. Instead, build rapport, make strong eye contact, mention possible consequences of telling lies (for example, loss of reputation), and then instead of telling the child not to lie, tell the child to tell you the truth (it's easier to process do's than don'ts.)

Gentle physical contact, along with eye contact can be a good way to establish rapport. A friendly hand on the shoulder or back can help you "connect."

One clever trick someone taught me is to frame the request this way: "You can trust me with the truth."

One mistake most parents make is to feel a need to rush a resolution. They get angry and impatient when the child stalls coming clean. It actually works better if you patiently make them sweat it out.

If they tell you another lie, or keep insisting the one they told you is true, DO NOT REACT, especially not emotionally. Just keep looking the child in the eye, say preferably nothing and in any case as little as possible, and wait for the truth to come out. The child is as anxious to resolve the tension as you are. Make the resolution depend on getting the truth out.

Child does something dangerous but without malicious intent.
Example: steps into traffic...runs and jumps towards picture-window pane...tries to swing from a live power line...climbs a

ladder and ends up on the roof, etc.

Many parents assume that the effectiveness of a punishment is directly proportional to its severity. They reason that they must severely punish the child if the stakes are high. For example it used to be fairly ubiquitous to spank small children for innocently wandering into the street.

What those parents are really doing is punishing the child for THE PARENTS' bad behavior. THEY failed to effectively train the child never to step into the street without an adult escort. There's likely a deficit of parental supervision going on.

In less common situations, like going up a ladder and climbing on the roof, the child apparently didn't anticipate being forbidden to do that any more than you would anticipate that the child would ever do that.

The way to fix these situations is to proactively teach the child about common dangers involving cars, electricity, fire, machinery, heights, dangerous animals, and dangerous people, and when situations were overlooked, or the lesson didn't stick, talk to them about it after the fact. Solicit and obtain an intention to comply. Give frequent reminders until the lesson sticks.

Child does something dangerous with malicious intent but without understanding consequences. For example, tries to get sibling to eat a toadstool without realizing that some are fatally poisonous.

Assign consequences. Afterwards, give a reprimand that includes an explanation of the dangers, and a requirement to apologize to the offended party.

Don't use euphemisms or understatements to describe danger. Don't say "That Angel-of-Death mushroom might make your tummy feel bad!" Describe danger as accurately as possible within the child's ability to understand. Don't blame the object of danger, like "did that bad kitty scratch you?" after the child pulled its tail. Encourage a sense of responsibility as well as a sense of cause-and-effect.

Child does something violent with malicious intent. Examples: kills the cat...tries to stab another child...steals other kids' lunch money...

Beyond the scope of this document. You can use the techniques described here, but they are unlikely to be enough; something is seriously wrong. Seek professional help before it progresses beyond your ability to handle it.

Appendix IV
Problem-solving techniques

There are so many techniques listed in this document that you might understandably have difficulty remembering them all, or knowing which ones are critically important. Importance is relative to where the deficits are. For example, if you are disorganized yourself, but not prone to criticizing, then providing structure might be relatively more important for you to focus your attention on.

Here is a short list of the most important techniques, in no particular order:

Take responsibility

Children's patterns of behavior are based on the experiences you have created for them to react to, and on your own reactions to their reactions. If one of your children has a problem behavior, you have to find a better way to respond to it than you have up to now. You need to change your own behavior first.

Supervise and give attention

There is no substitute for giving children your time and attention. If you can't, you need to find another responsible adult willing and able to do so, whom you have carefully vetted. As long as you stay alert to trouble and calm when you react to it, supervision is in itself enough to prevent most problems. Obviously, you're at work for most of the day. When you're home, assume that you're in charge.

You also need to monitor the interactions between your children and other sources of attention, be they people or electronics.

Negotiate understandings before trouble

The heat of the moment is the worst possible time to talk about a problem and negotiate a resolution. Either anticipate problems before they happen and negotiate an understanding regarding how your child will respond to the situation, or, lacking foresight, save the negotiation for when you and your child are calm and can work out an understanding to at least avoid a repeat. Children can usually stick to plan as long as there is one, and it's specific enough for them to mentally model it ("be good" won't do it). During the heat of the moment, keep the discussion to a minimum.

Understand perspectives

Seek to understand children's motives and points of view. The child is just seeking pleasure (sometimes in the wrong places) and avoiding pain, which are the same motivations you have too.

Right now there are a lot of self-centered, inconsiderate behaviors among younger generations. Psychologists call it an "epidemic of narcissism." For this reason it's important that you also teach empathy for other people's perspectives, compassion for their feelings, and respect for their rights. Ask children to consider how other people feel about the consequences of their behavior, both good and bad. It's important for children to make the leap from "don't do that because I'm bigger than you" to "don't do that because it hurts other people."

Establish positive rapport

Positive rapport is so important that all by itself it would solve most behavioral problems. When you are in rapport with a child, the child is listening to you; when you are out of rapport, the child is not listening to you. Give your full attention to the child and get his or hers. Connect heart-to-heart. Get down on the child's eye level, and maintain steady eye contact. If you're in a conversation with the child regarding a problem, don't totally dominate it, and do actively listen. Patiently wait for answers and expressions of commitment. Pay attention to exactly what the child is saying, and also to the child's emotional state.

Boys are slightly harder to get into rapport than girls are. Just pay a little more attention to where their attention is, and be a little more patient.

Maintain a stable, calm, rational mood

Kids aren't messed up by learning to face the consequences of their behaviors; they're messed up by learning to react to problems with rage or terror, both of which cloud rational judgment. If you calmly deal with the situation, you will maintain a good rapport with your kids and teach them to deal with problems rationally.

The question is how do you stay calm when a child has just done something destructive or irritating.

One way is to know how to defuse minor situations before they escalate. The typical pattern of escalation won't happen if you promptly interrupt misbehavior by issuing a strike or consequences.

But not all problems are escalations; sometimes there's a big mess on your hands before you had an opportunity to interrupt misbehavior. Telling yourself to stay calm and rational isn't going to do it. But if you do get angry, ask yourself if anger is going to help the situation, or make it worse.

The purpose of anger is to get you ready for a fight. Are you going to physically attack your own children as if they were an existential threat to you? Chances are, they're not, and your anger is irrational. Save your fighting mood for real threats and don't allow it to trigger against those you love.

Once you convince yourself that anger isn't serving you, ask yourself to let it go. More generally, train yourself to become aware of your emotional state, and get into the habit of asking yourself if your emotion is serving you, or making things worse.

Also get into the habit of quickly coming to terms with things outside of your control. You sigh, and tell yourself: "So it is." Once you come to terms with things, ask yourself: "What's the next step?"

If you make this change in your ability to control your emotions, your kids won't be the only ones to benefit. So will you. The ability to make conscious, intelligent choices regarding your own emotions, so that you manage them instead of them managing you, takes your life to the next level.

Appendix IV: Problem-solving techniques

Interrupt misbehavior and give feedback

You need to interrupt misbehavior promptly, to prevent or disrupt bad habits and to keep from losing your own temper. Feedback helps children stay on track. You need to deliver it in a way that does not distract their attention from what they should be doing, or trigger unhelpful emotions like anger or fear. Use "3 strikes" as your default method of giving feedback for minor offenses from the ages of about 3 or 4 through 12. On the third strike, back it up with non-violent sanctions.

Use this formula to issue reprimands:

- establish rapport
- recall the behavior and the trouble it caused
- state a rule expressed in simple and specific language (if-then language is good) that will prevent a recurrence
- solicit and wait for a firm commitment to comply with the rule

Help children manage their attention

Encourage children to plan their own activities to the ability they've built up to. Give them plenty of active-attention activities and projects to work on.

Don't criticize

Criticism is punishment for obedience, however half-hearted or inadequate. Criticism is not telling children what to do; it's telling them what they did wrong in a personal, negative way. Give feedback in a way that directs attention to a child's behavior rather than to the child's sense-of-self.

Provide structure

Don't take your own lack of adequate organization out on your kids. It's not their fault, and they're not going to learn to be organized themselves except through your leadership by example.

Structure includes schedules and specific family rules. Having specific rules creates a sense of order instead of "dad bossing us around."

Structure can include props that help children remember rules. For example, a teddy bear might remind a child to sit quietly for a quiet activity, a personalized mat might remind a child to sit in one spot instead of jumping up and running around, and a timer might help time-management.

Appendix V
Sample family rules

Here is a sample list of family rules that you can use as a basis for coming up with your own list. It covers only a few basics, and you will probably want to add a few of your own. I did add a few safety rules, but safety is a whole other topic that would require its own book to do it justice.

Notice that several of the rules are expressed in "if (condition) then..." language. There are also patterns like "...when (condition) and "...unless (condition)", which are similar; the point is to specify a triggering condition, often in the form of a place or type of event. That kind of language is easier for the brain to process.

- Don't go anywhere unless we know about it.
- Don't go anywhere with anyone you don't know.
- Don't go anywhere with anyone we don't know.

- Answer words with words, not fists.
- Tell others what you want, not what you think is wrong with them.
- Use respectful language.
- Use a respectful tone of voice.

- If it's not yours, then ask before using or handling it.

- If you make a mess, then clean it up before starting another activity.

- If it's time to come to the dinner table, then finish what you are doing and put it away.
- If you don't like what you are being served at the table, then limit your remarks to "no thank you", especially at other people's homes.
- If you want to leave the dinner table, first ask to be excused.

Good luck enforcing limits on computer time. Teachers often make these limits hard to enforce by explicitly assigning computer time, as if kids won't learn how to use a computer if the teachers don't assign them computer-based homework.

The two-hour limit on activities that involve electronics is an absolute maximum. Your children would benefit from having active-attention activities that displace their passive-attention activities in the first place. Make a habit of taking them outside to play with them.

- Confirm your homework is ready to turn in before using the computer for fun and games.
- No more than 2 hours daily maximum time with electronics. That includes assigned homework on the computer.
- No television, computer, or other electronic devices on Sundays (dopamine detox day).

Good behavior implies good manners. Good manners are based on consideration for others, and a friendly attitude. The best way to teach good manners is by example. To cover enough examples to do it justice, I'd need to write another book. Here are just a few examples to get started:

- If you want a favor, then remember to say "please".
- If someone has given you a gift or favor, then say "thank you".
- If someone you want to talk to is in the company of someone you don't know or don't intend to talk to, greet both of them anyway. Don't make people feel like they are not worthy of your attention.
- If you meet someone you know while you are in the company of someone that person doesn't know, introduce the two strangers to each other. If you're not sure whether they know each or not, ask.
- If you need the attention of someone who is busy, say "excuse me for interrupting".
- If someone else's door is closed, then knock on it before entering.

Moral judgments aren't innate; they're learned. People often assume they're innate, because they're learned unconsciously, but people in different times and places have had extremely different senses of morality. As of this writing, there's a moral crisis unfolding, whereby there's no workable consensus on even very basic moral judgments, because people are no longer consistently learning any moral rules at all, much less the same ones.

Here's a simple rule, of Christian origin, that at least sets things in the right direction:

Treat other people the way you would like them to treat you.

It's the golden rule expressed in modern English. There's another rule that's not quite as ubiquitously known:

Treat other people the way they treat you.

The combination of the two rules, with the first rule applying to new relationships so that you can bootstrap cooperation, is a rough approximation of the tit-for-tat strategy from game theory.

An obstacle to practicing the second rule: life isn't fair, there are double-standards everywhere, some people have more brute power than you do, and there are many circumstances in which you'll get into more trouble than you can handle if you actually do treat people the way they treat you.

But who says you have to respond in-kind? Rarely are you ever totally powerless—and if you were, you're probably dependent too and in that case it's on you that you have to dance to someone else's tune. Use whatever freedom of choice remains to you.

"I'm taking my ball and going home."

Bonus report
First steps in learning at home

As I write this, most families rely on wage income from both dads and moms. As a result, "homeschooling" seems out-of-reach to most parents. And yet I am surprised how often someone asks me about what the commitment of time and money would be like. It usually happens after a school mass shooting, or a video makes the rounds revealing some sort of shocking political or sexual indoctrination. UPDATE 2021: During the covid-19 pandemic, it's happening a lot because of utter chaos in the schools. UPDATE 2022: OK, now I'm shocked and horrified at the grooming videos showing up on social media, and I imagine that so are a lot of you readers! I've long been aware that there have been problems, but now it looks like some teachers, often with the backing of their school systems, are ignoring any and all boundaries.

The question of commitment is hard to answer, because it depends on a lot of variables. If you "think outside the box," it can be arranged with varying levels of costs and benefits. If one parent can arrange to work at home, it can be easier and more fun than sending them to institutionalized school. If one or more grandparents are available and are willing to participate (actually, sometimes it's their idea), it can be arranged. I've recently read a flurry of social media posts from Afroamerican parents bluntly stating: "don't tell me I can't do this; I already am! I'm not rich, but I'm determined."

One of the biggest obstacles is purely conceptual: the word "homeschooling" suggests a parent standing in front of a blackboard, lecturing like a school-marm. It works better if you DON'T lecture them; that paradigm is a legacy of the days when books were expensive, so the teacher had the only copy and read it aloud to the class. Most of the time, the students read their own lessons and work on them, preferably at their own pace, since the only reason for keeping all the students at the same pace (before it started turning into a goal in itself), was for the teacher's sake, not the students'.

That said, there are some educational activities that are worth doing together if for no other reasons than parent-child bonding time and fun. There's also the matter of jumpstarting the process by teaching how to learn. Learning how to learn, by the way, is something they'll never get in school.

How about if I offer a few easy projects for beginning learners to inspire you, and you can decide what, if anything, you want to do with them? I have a much longer list, a whole book actually, but the content would overwhelm this book. SOME learning should happen at home, regardless of where your children do most of their learning.

By the way, because schools in some countries, particularly the English-speaking ones, are not very effective, learning some basics at home is your children's best shot at learning anything useful at all.

This also means you've got a low standard to beat.

Bonus report: First steps in learning at home

UPDATE 2020: Now that lockdowns are an ongoing possibility, learning at home is more important than it used to be. Get the basics down, and don't obsess over how it compares to formal institutional education.

Counting

Let's start with counting. It works better if you count actual items: pine cones, sea-shells, pebbles, pennies, marbles, autumnal leaves, whatever. Your counters should all be the same type of item. Collecting the items to count can be its own fun activity.

What I used to do is use the counters as representations for items or characters in a story:

> "One little chicken went out looking for worms to eat. Another little chicken joined her and now there are two little chickens out looking for worms. Another little chicken joined them and now there are three little chickens out looking for worms."

My kids loved these stories. Mistakes were corrected on the fly by simply repeating back correct answers:

> "How many chickens are there?"
> "One-two-three chickens!"
> "That's right, there are three chickens."

It took maybe a week to get to ten, and then several more to get to twenty. Numbers that break patterns, like eleven, twelve, and to a certain degree thirteen, are a little harder than numbers that follow patterns.

How to teach the alphabet

Teach the **sounds** of the letters before teaching the names of the letters. Don't push the names of the letters; they're not all that important. Teaching the names of the letters before and instead of teaching their sounds turns into an impediment for reading:

Parent: Read this word: cat.
Child: see-ay-tee

A busy-body insisted that I'm wrong and taught one of my daughters the NAMES of the letters in the alphabet behind my back and against my wishes. It took me several weeks to get her to pronounce the sounds of the letters instead of the names.

Instead, teach children the closest thing to the SOUND(S) of the letter. Associate the SOUND the letter represents to the letter, instead of its name, which is close to useless when they're just learning letters.

Most teachers seem to disagree with me about this. But I seem to be able to teach three and four-year-olds how to read, whereas nowadays teachers are struggling to teach seven and eight-year-olds to read, and at a much slower pace at that. The teachers might say "well, you've only got one at a time; I have a whole classroom," to which I would say "you're getting paid to give them your whole attention for many hours each week; I'm not and I have other responsibilities to take care of."

When to teach kids to read

Here are the signs I would look for that a child might be ready to learn to read:

- They talk freely in complete sentences.
- They enjoy stories.
- They enjoy being read to, often initiate the activity, and maintain their attention on the pictures in books when you read to them.
- They have a sense of which way is the right way to hold the book (not upside-down), and an intuitive sense of the significance of turning the pages (they might even turn the pages themselves in their eagerness to see the next page).

Once we start the process of learning how to read, I look for confirmation that it's easy and enjoyable. If they're struggling or hate it, it's either too early or paced too fast. If they have an impediment to reading, then it will manifest in some sort of difficulty. Just pay attention to feedback and respond accordingly.

My own kids seemed to be ready between the ages of three to four. I kept the lessons quite short, about ten or fifteen minutes, because kids in that age range have short attention spans. There are a lot of variables, so results will vary. Don't sweat it; enjoy it!

How to teach kids to read

When I read to kids who haven't learned to read yet, or who are just starting to read, I run my finger under the words as I read them. I assume that it helps train them to track with their eyes.

I tried all sorts of methods and books before I found this one, which was the most effective and is now my go-to resource:

The reading lesson: Teach your child to read in 20 easy lessons
by Michael Levin, MD and Charan Langton MS
Published by Mountcastle Company

Despite the reference to "lessons," each one of those is long enough that you're going to want to break them up. I did single daily sessions of about ten to fifteen minutes each with my youngest daughter, over the course of five months when she was four years old.

Finding other books to read once this one is finished is harder, but only because too many unsuitable books make it hard to find the good ones. You will quickly discover that most early-reading books have ridiculously small type for a child. It's because the publishers assume that kids can't read. Often enough, the publishers don't seem to have a clear idea regarding whether a book is designed to be read by a child or an adult, and send mixed-messages with their inconsistencies. Another common problem is mismatches in interest levels, as the publishers will assume that kids who can read are at least seven, more likely eight years old.

You'll also discover that a lot of contemporary children's fiction is political and social indoctrination, forget about learning to read. Some parents try to avoid the problem by looking for older classics, but often enough they're trading one set of problems for another.

I don't have a solution, other than filtering out anything particularly bad, and paying attention and making the best of the rest. When I read a book with my younger daughter, we stop and talk about things whenever we run into a problem.

Have fun!

How to help other readers

Book reviews help readers decide if a book is worth their time and money. You benefit when other people take the time to write thoughtful reviews of books you're considering for purchase. If this book was useful to you, you could pass the favor forward to other readers by submitting a book review on the website where you bought it.

If you have suggestions for improving the book, you can look for the author's handle, @KalkinTrivedi, on social media. Engage him publically before attempting to contact him privately, otherwise your message will get lost among the spam. Your thoughtful feedback and your time to write it up are valuable and appreciated.

Credits

Stock photo images and fonts are the property of their owners and are used under license.

© iStock / gradyreese

The display font is HiLo Deco, used under SIL Open Font License. The body-copy font is Gentium Plus, used under SIL Open Font License. Dingbats are Noto Emoji, used under Open Font License.

www.ingramcontent.com/pod-product-compliance
Lightning Source LLC
LaVergne TN
LVHW020925090426
835512LV00020B/3210